CALEDONIAN IN LMS I

Niall Ferguson and David Stirling

CONTENTS

Introduction

There have been surprisingly few books written about the Caledonian Railway and even fewer about its existence under the London Midland & Scottish Railway. There are, of course, a fair number of line histories, the majority of which cover the LMS era, and there is an active Line Society with a regular Journal which covers all periods up to, and including, Nationalisation. However, as one of the two large Scottish pre-grouping companies, and the largest Scottish company to enter the LMS group, the lack of published works is somewhat surprising. The Caledonian Railway undoubtedly became the dominant partner in the LMS Northern Division; its locomotive classes spread throughout the lines of the other LMS constituents north of the border and were often of sufficient quality to prevent the influx of the LMS standard designs seen elsewhere (certainly as far as freight traffic and secondary passenger services were concerned).

The authors hope that this volume will go some way to redressing that lack. Obviously in a relatively short volume we have had to be selective about mixing what we consider to be important with those aspects of more general interest, but we trust that the reader will get a view of the breadth of LMS operations on the former Caledonian Railway together with the changes that occurred during the 25 years of LMS control, and some of the reasons for those changes.

Former CR '812' Class 0-6-0 No.17588 (CR 850) at Aberdeen on Wednesday 22nd June 1927. Despite the locomotive's having been repainted in LMS livery, it is coupled to the tender from No.859 of the same class, which is still in Caledonian livery. No.859 was a Westinghouse-fitted locomotive, so the tender is painted in Caledonian blue (confirmed by the presence of the company crest) and would have been a considerable contrast to the black livery of the locomotive. (H. C. Casserley)

This volume would not have been possible without the assistance of many of our friends, both within the LMS Society and the Caledonian Railway Association, and outside. Although we owe a debt to all of them, we would like to mention in particular, John Burnie, Hamish Stevenson, David Hamilton, Stuart Rankin, Jim MacIntosh, and Nelson Twells. We are grateful to the National Archives (formerly the Public Record Office) at Kew, the National Archives of Scotland and to their helpful staff for access to their extensive records and to the Scottish Railway Preservation Society. Photographs are also difficult to choose, especially finding some that have not previously been seen. Although we both have fairly extensive photographic collections to draw from, we are indebted to the many sources from which they have been acquired over the

A 15-ton mineral wagon exhibiting the seamless transition from CR to LMS, with both numbers and set of initials visible. (Jim MacIntosh's Collection)

years. We have tried, where possible, to credit the original photographer, and are particularly grateful to Richard Casserley and Hamish Stevenson for their permission to use photographs from their own and their late fathers' collections.

Whilst we are, obviously, indebted to those mentioned above, the opinions and any errors in the volume are our personal responsibility.

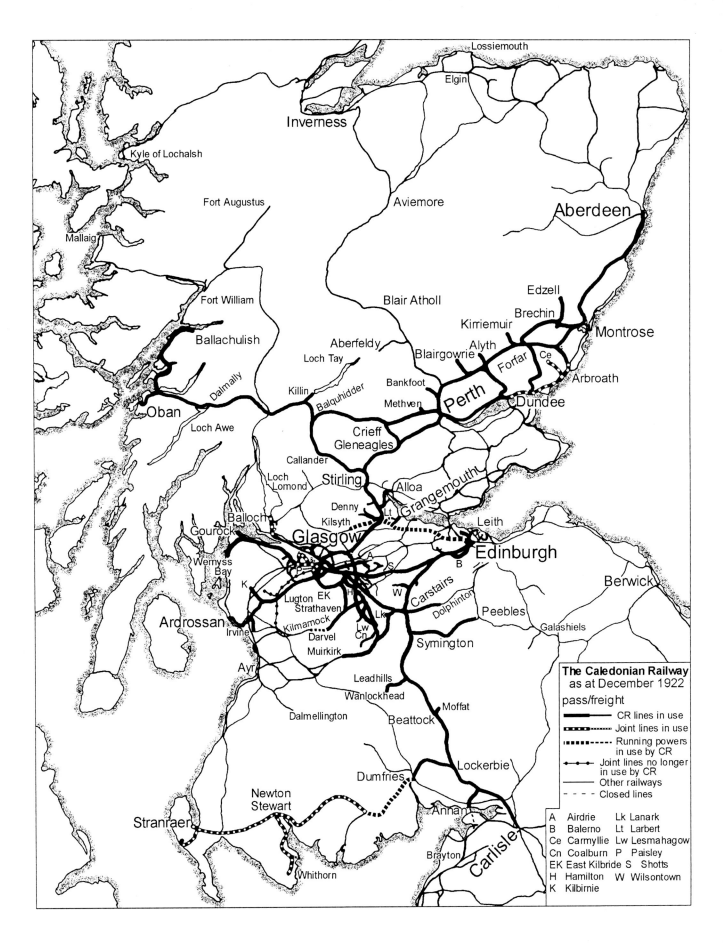

The Caledonian Railway as at December 1922

pass/freight

- CR lines in use
- Joint lines in use
- Running powers in use by CR
- Joint lines no longer in use by CR
- Other railways
- Closed lines

A	Airdrie
B	Balerno
Ce	Carmyllie
Cn	Coalburn
EK	East Kilbride
H	Hamilton
K	Kilbirnie
Lk	Lanark
Lt	Larbert
Lw	Lesmahagow
P	Paisley
S	Shotts
W	Wilsontown

Lossiemouth, Elgin, Inverness, Kyle of Lochalsh, Mallaig, Fort Augustus, Aviemore, Aberdeen, Fort William, Ballachulish, Blair Atholl, Edzell, Brechin, Kirriemuir, Montrose, Alyth, Aberfeldy, Blairgowrie, Forfar, Ce, Loch Tay, Bankfoot, Dalmally, Killin, Methven, Perth, Dundee, Arbroath, Oban, Balquhidder, Loch Awe, Crieff, Gleneagles, Callander, Loch Lomond, Stirling, Alloa, Grangemouth, Denny, Kilsyth, Lt, Leith, Balloch, Gourock, Glasgow, Edinburgh, Wemyss Bay, K, A, S, B, Berwick, Lugton, EK, Strathaven, H, W, Carstairs, Ardrossan, Kilmarnock, Lk, Dolphinton, Peebles, Irvine, Darvel, Lw, Cn, Galashiels, Muirkirk, Symington, Ayr, Leadhills, Wanlockhead, Moffat, Dalmellington, Beattock, Lockerbie, Dumfries, Newton Stewart, Annan, Stranraer, Brayton, Carlisle, Whithorn

4

1

Origins

Of the Scottish railway companies which joined the LMS in 1923 the Caledonian was by far the largest with 1,114.4 route miles of track (not including sidings), as well as 1,077 locomotives, 3,040 coaches (including Non Passenger Coaching Stock [NPCS]), 51,536 freight and 1,786 service vehicles, and vied with the North British Railway (which joined the LNER) for being the largest of all the Scottish railway companies.

The Caledonian Railway opened its main line from Carlisle to Glasgow over Beattock, with a branch to Edinburgh which left the main line at Carstairs, in 1848. Having been planned in conjunction with the Grand Junction 'group' of companies, the Caledonian usually worked closely with the Scottish Central Railway (which ran from Greenhill to Perth) and Scottish North Eastern Railway (from Perth to Aberdeen) and, following a series of amalgamations in the 1860s, emerged as the pre-eminent west coast company in Scotland, with major stations in Glasgow, Edinburgh, Stirling, Perth, Dundee and Aberdeen. A further acquisition of the Wemyss Bay line in 1865, and of the working of the Caledonian-promoted Callander and Oban Railway in 1870 (not opened throughout until 1880), gave it access to a large proportion of the west coast of Scotland, and joint ownership of the Portpatrick and Wigtownshire Railway (in conjunction with the London & North Western, Midland and Glasgow & South Western Railways) gave access to Stranraer and the Irish ferries. It even had a second, although very subsidiary, line into England over the Solway Viaduct. Although these amalgamations had produced what to the general public appeared as a single entity, legally there were still a number of small independent railway companies within the Caledonian Railway's area of operation, over whose rails the larger company operated the train service.

Following the Great War there was a considerable debate on the possible re-organisation of the various British railway companies. Although nationalisation was considered, in June 1920 a proposal was made to amalgamate the various companies into seven groups, one of which was to cover Scotland and include all the Scottish companies (as actually occurred with the railway nationalisation of 1948). Further consideration, however, led to the view that a Scottish group would lack financial strength, and the final scheme produced four groups of which two, the London & North Eastern Railway (LNER) and London Midland and Scottish Railway (LMS), would reach into Scotland, the Caledonian Railway joining the Highland and Glasgow & South Western Railways in the LMS Group, whilst the North British and Great North of Scotland Railways joined the LNER, a scheme sanctioned by the Railways Act of 1921 and which came into effect on 1st January 1923.

The final years of the nineteenth century had seen the Caledonian institute a series of major improvements to many of its larger stations, the most notable of these being to Glasgow Central station, but unfortunately the same was not true for other aspects of its operations. As far as carriages were concerned, the Caledonian Railway had found that the financial constraints imposed during the Great War had resulted in massive delays in the replacement of coaching stock. In 1913 the average life expectancy of a carriage (its age at its removal from capital stock, not necessarily the same as its being scrapped or sold) was 32 years; by 1919 that age had risen to 40 years. The LMS took over 2,315 passenger carriages from the Caledonian in 1923. That figure even included a small number of vehicles which pre-dated Dugald Drummond's appointment as Caledonian Locomotive Superintendent in 1882, and also contained a considerable number of four and six-wheel carriages which had been built by Drummond and his successors, principally John Farquharson McIntosh (Hugh Smellie and John Lambie not being in post long enough to have made a significant impact on carriage design or numbers).

The first Caledonian bogie vehicles (apart from six 49ft-long carriages of 1886 which were intended to run in two matching rakes of three) were 45ft long and 8ft wide, and were essentially longer versions of Drummond's 35ft six-wheelers. Initially McIntosh was content to continue the construction of these 35ft and 45ft carriages which had effectively been designed by Drummond up to fifteen years previously, but before long he lengthened the 45ft carriages designs to 48ft, thus increasing the amount of leg room in the compartments, and then increased their width from 8 feet to 8ft 6in. The latter increase, as well as providing yet more room for passengers, allowed space for a side corridor, thus simplifying the provision of lavatory facilities; corridor connections

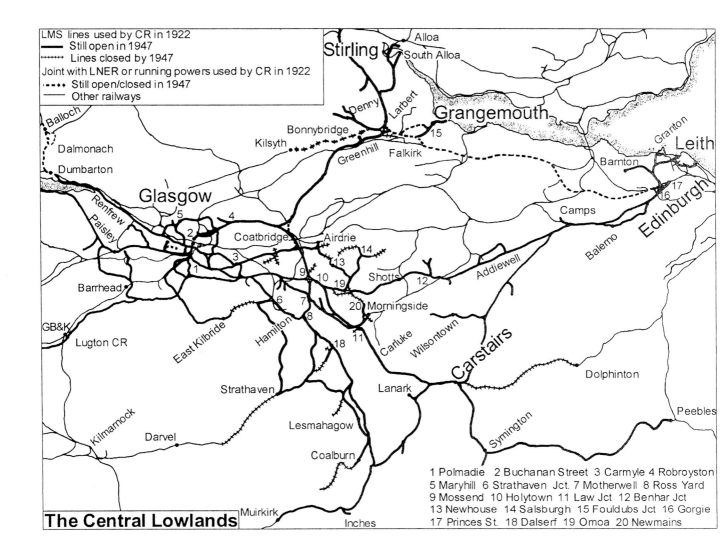

LMS lines used by CR in 1922
——— Still open in 1947
+++++++ Lines closed by 1947
Joint with LNER or running powers used by CR in 1922
•-•••• Still open/closed in 1947
——— Other railways

The Central Lowlands

1 Polmadie 2 Buchanan Street 3 Carmyle 4 Robroyston
5 Maryhill 6 Strathaven Jct. 7 Motherwell 8 Ross Yard
9 Mossend 10 Holytown 11 Law Jct 12 Benhar Jct
13 Newhouse 14 Salsburgh 15 Fouldubs Jct 16 Gorgie
17 Princes St. 18 Dalserf 19 Omoa 20 Newmains

Inches

between adjoining carriages were, however, still absent. Then, in 1904, McIntosh brought the Caledonian right up to date with the introduction of the 65ft long and 9ft wide 'Grampian' corridor carriages on six-wheel bogies, which eventually included both corridor and non-corridor designs , some non-corridor third class vehicles being 68ft long. In the first years of the new century a few coaches of 50ft length were produced for use on the Oban line, which had restrictions which prevented the use of the 65ft stock, further examples of the same length being produced over the following years. Then, in 1910, McIntosh produced the first examples of a 57ft carriage, a length which became standard for the rest of the Caledonian Railway's separate existence and was also to be adopted as a standard length by the LMS.

Until 1914 the only vehicles with dining facilities that were to be found on the Caledonian (with the exception of a very rudimentary gas ring on the occasional saloon carriage) belonged either to the West Coast Joint Stock (WCJS), a pool of carriages jointly owned by the Caledonian and LNWR companies, or those owned solely by the LNWR; in fact the Caledonian had to borrow an LNWR dining car to use on the opening trip of the prestigious 'Grampian Corridor Express' in 1904. Then, in 1905, it received four ex-WCJS dining vehicles from the twelve withdrawn in that year to make way for new stock. Those remained the only Caledonian-owned restaurant cars for the following nine years, running between Perth and Carlisle or between Glasgow and Aberdeen.

However, in 1912 the Caledonian began negotiations with the Pullman Car Company for the provision of seventeen vehicles (originally intended to be thirteen buffet cars and four dining cars). The Pullman cars were to be built at the expense of the Pullman company and owned by it, and Pullman would be remunerated both by the profits it made from catering and by charging a supplementary fare in the case of the buffet cars, and solely by profits from catering in the case of the dining cars: the Caledonian Railway would be responsible for the cost of hauling the vehicles, but no other costs would be borne by the railway company. The thirteen carriages were intended to

Waiting for the road. Drummond '66' Class 4-4-0 No.1091 in Caledonian livery at Edinburgh Princes Street about 1923. This locomotive was withdrawn soon afterwards and never carried an LMS number. Notice the Pullman car being watered in the background and the end of the massive signal gantry. The surroundings of the operational part of Princes Street station, with tenements and industrial premises forming the backdrop, were much less impressive than the frontage.
(J. J. Cunningham)

enter service in June 1914 but by the outbreak of war in that month only ten had been delivered, of which eight were in service. The Pullman services were all withdrawn at the end of 1916 (a decision resulting in a successful financial dispute with the Government) but were returned to service at the beginning of March 1919. Further contracts with the Pullman company were signed that year extending the agreement until 1933, and by the end of 1922 thirteen cars (although not identical to those originally intended) had been delivered to the Caledonian, still four short of the number contracted. The fact that the Caledonian did not officially join the LMS until six months later meant that the Pullman company officially

fulfilled its order with the original company when it delivered a further four cars in May 1923.

From the late 1880s the Caledonian Railway had operated steamer services on the Clyde Coast in the persona of its wholly owned subsidiary, the Caledonian Steam Packet Co. (CSPC). This had been in competition with the NBR and the G&SWR, as well as with a number of smaller private boats. During the Great War all the Caledonian boats had eventually been requisitioned for war service and in order to maintain a service the company had been forced to charter vessels from other companies and, in addition, during wartime conditions the three railway fleets were operated as a single unit.

*No.17339 on an Oban–Stirling cattle train ascending the bank to Glencruitten, assisted in the rear by a banking engine. The climb to Glencruitten summit was very steep (1 in 50) on either side, that from Oban being the more taxing as the engines were starting cold. In 1887 this became the first section in Britain to be protected by a banking token, allowing the banker to assist in section as far as the summit and return to Oban Junction, without going through the section to Connel Ferry. This arrangement became redundant when the crossing loop at Glencruitten was opened in 1903. (*LCGB Ken Nunn Collection)

Two Caledonian steamers (*Duchess of Hamilton* and *Duchess of Montrose*) were sunk during the war, but the remainder returned to the Clyde during 1919. By 1920 all ships were back in operation, but were used as a pool with the other two companies, the same happening in 1921 and 1922. Although offered compensation for the vessels it had lost, the company had been financially damaged by the war, particularly by the fact that no payment was made for the requisitioned vessels which returned, nor for the cost of chartering replacements.

As with the majority of British railway companies, the Great War had left the Caledonian in a parlous state. The company's rolling stock and locomotives had not been replaced for some years, and a scheme of renovation commenced. A renewal programme was initiated in January 1918 under which no fewer than 41 locomotives were to be constructed by the end of 1919. The same programme addressed the carriage stock as well, it having been found that there was also an urgent need to replace a large number of outdated carriages. Although the company owned 2,092 carriages, only 17 fewer than in 1913, in 1913 nearly 600 of those vehicles had been built in the previous twenty years, and a mere 52 were over 40 years old. By 1918 fewer than 600 carriages had been built in the previous 20 years, and the number over 40 years old had risen to 161, including a substantial number dating back to the 1870s. Not a single new carriage had been built since 1916, leaving a shortfall of no fewer than 161 which should have been built between then and December 1919, without taking into account the sixteen modern bogie carriages which had been transferred to the British Expeditionary Force in France to form Continental Ambulance Train No.21, and which were not returned.

Not only was there a serious lack of modern carriages but, of those 2,092 coaches, only 585 were fitted with steam heating, i.e. about 28%, and only 93 carriages had been so fitted since 1911. Wagon stock too was in a similar state, with the construction of no fewer than 1,610 new wagons having been delayed by the war, of which over 1,000 would have been 16-ton capacity mineral wagons. That shortage was made worse by the fact that nearly 3,500 private owner wagons had been withdrawn since 1914 and a recommendation was made that 2,800 new wagons were needed, of which over 2,000 should be 16-ton mineral wagons.

Fortunately the Caledonian Railway's directors had put aside money for that unbuilt rolling stock, the fund available for wagons and carriages in 1919 standing at £461,727. The rate of inflation during the war meant, however, that such a seemingly large amount of money was still nowhere near sufficient and, even if it had been, there were insufficient suppliers to enable such large orders to be filled. It was therefore decided that forty 57ft bogie carriages would be ordered at a cost of £253,000 (only £49,848 having been set aside) and 550 wagons of various types at a cost of £189,000 (although no fewer than 730 wagons were eventually ordered).

As stated above, the Great War caused almost a complete hiatus in the construction of new vehicles and, although between 1918 and 1923 further carriages of both 57ft and 50ft length were constructed, both by the Caledonian and by outside builders, the company joined the LMS with a dearth of new carriages and a preponderance of elderly vehicles overdue for replacement. Some of those vehicles had been built as long ago as 1889, and hardly any carried, or were even allocated, their LMS numbers. All of those ancient carriages (fewer than a hundred) had disappeared by the end of 1925, along with nearly 150 four-wheel carriages which had been built by Dugald Drummond. The only place where four-wheel carriages were still to be seen was on the Balerno and Leith branches in Edinburgh where the tight curves meant that 39 four-wheel coaches built as recently as 1920 were still to be seen right through the LMS period, not finally being withdrawn until 1952.

The formation of the LMSR in 1923 found the Caledonian, like the North Staffordshire Railway south of the border, in a financial dispute with the new company. That was because the number of shares in the LMSR that were allotted to shareholders in the constituent companies in return for their existing shares was calculated on the basis of the constituent company's profits for the year 1913. That year had been chosen as the last complete one before the outbreak of the Great War, but the Caledonian and North Staffordshire directors argued that 1913 had been an unusually bad year for their respective companies, and therefore did not reflect their true financial worth. In 1913 the Caledonian had declared a dividend of only 3½% compared with the LNWR one of 7% and it was not until the result of arbitration was announced in June 1923 that matters were finalised. As a result neither company joined the LMS in January 1923, waiting instead until 1st July 1923 to formally merge. The composition of the new LMS Board, with only two of its 26 members coming from the Caledonian Railway (Henry Allan, the Caledonian's Chairman, and William Younger), compared with no fewer than twenty from the LNWR and Midland Railway, left little doubt as to where policy would originate. Notwithstanding the six months' delay, and although their representatives would not join the LMS Board until July, the directors of the still nominally independent Caledonian, realising that it was only a matter of time before acceptable financial terms were agreed, generally behaved as part of the new conglomerate from the beginning of 1923, and a Scottish Committee of the LMS was founded as the result of a meeting at Euston on 15th December 1922. The Scottish Committee held its first meeting a week

In the mid-1920s a Drummond 4-4-0, still in Caledonian livery and fitted with Westinghouse brake but no vacuum, hauls a mixed freight headed by some coaching vehicles northwards out of the yard at Balhousie, at the north end of Perth. The yards stretched from here past Dovecoteland into Perth itself. The industrial hinterland and tenement houses are evocative of the later nineteenth and early twentieth century landscape in industrial Scotland, and testify that Perth was more than just a railway centre. (J. J. Cunningham)

later, taking over complete responsibility for management of the former G&SWR and Highland Railways, but with partial responsibility for, and considerable influence over, matters on the Caledonian section.

It was, of course, not only the composition of the LMS Board that reflected the MR and LNWR's controlling interest; of the ten Chief Officers appointed in January 1923, only Donald Matheson of the Caledonian, who became Manager for Scotland, was not a former employee of the Midland, LNWR or Lancashire & Yorkshire Railway.

However, below that level the Caledonian was better represented: the Chief General Superintendent (responsible for the railway's day-to-day operations) might have been J. H. Follows of the Midland, but two of his three deputies, the General Superintendents, were former Caledonian men, with J. Ballantyne taking charge of the Northern Division (Scotland) whilst R. Killin was given charge of the Midland Division. On the locomotive side, although the Caledonian's Locomotive Superintendent, William Pickersgill, was appointed Divisional Mechanical Engineer at St. Rollox, he was 63 years of age, and retired to Bournemouth in 1925. Pickersgill was succeeded in Scotland by another former Caledonian employee, John G. Barr, CR Assistant Superintendent Running, who became Divisional Superintendent Motive Power, and who managed to maintain the Caledonian's influence despite J. E. Anderson, former Deputy C.M.E. of the Midland Railway, being appointed Superintendent of Motive Power. As Barr later said to O.S. Nock, "Euston was a long way away!"

LMS

2

Geography and Infrastructure

The LMS Inheritance

The railways were grouped in 1923 partly as a reaction to their weakened position after the 1914-18 war. When the LMS began the former Caledonian Railway became the dominant part of the Northern Division of the new undertaking, not just in the physical sense but perhaps more importantly in that many of the key posts in the new organisation were filled by Caley men. However, the very need for the grouping showed that things could not simply continue as they had done. So what was the place of the Caledonian section in the new undertaking?

The main lines of the CR were clear, from Carlisle through the central industrial belt to Perth and Aberdeen. These were what the caused the railway to be built in the first place, a good trunk route extending the West Coast Route northwards from the border, by the shortest rather than the most populated route, to the industrial lowlands. The Anglo-Scottish traffic flowed between the border and the Clyde Valley, with significantly less taking the offshoot towards Edinburgh. Diminishing amounts of traffic, joined by internal Scottish flows to and from the central belt, continued northwards to Stirling, Perth and beyond. Although Anglo-Scottish traffic was important, it was in the central belt that the core of the CR's business lay, with a dense passenger service,

The staff and a couple of young onlookers admire Lambie 4-4-0T No.15027, more than adequately provided with coal for the occasion, on arrival at Annan (Shawhill) with a very short mixed train from Kirtlebridge in the 1920s. The station may be near closure but is kept in very presentable condition adorned, as usual, by some milk churns. The access over a pedestrian portion of the overbridge through the gate in the roadside bridge parapet is distinctly unusual.
(J. J. Cunningham)

No.17908, of the '179' Class, shunting cattle wagons in the up loop at Lockerbie station signal box, while a down through train approaches in the distance. This locomotive, despite belonging to a small class, survived from 1914 until 1946. As can be seen from the row of cattle wagons in the background, and the staging for cleaning them, Lockerbie was something of a centre for this sort of traffic. This signal box took over control of the whole station in 1935, before which there were other boxes at the south end of the loop (in the distance) and at the north end behind the photographer. (J. J. Cunningham)

both commuter and longer distance, together with the mineral traffic. Freight and minerals had provided the bulk (58%) of the CR's traffic, the mineral business being largely in connection with the coal, steel and other heavy industries of the lowlands.

Apart from the trunk lines, the south of Scotland contributed relatively little to the Caledonian section of the LMS. There had been a line across the Solway from Kirtlebridge to Brayton on the Maryport & Carlisle Railway, built in the unfulfilled expectation of iron ore traffic from Cumberland to the west of Scotland. The viaduct across the Solway had been closed by the CR in 1921 and the main remnant was a branch from Kirtlebridge to Annan. The Abbey Junction–Brayton section, isolated from the rest of the CR, was still open for goods traffic (and some passenger excursions) but not worked by the Caledonian itself. From Lockerbie there was a more successful branch through agricultural country to Dumfries, which also functioned as the access to Galloway. The CR had once operated the Portpatrick Railway from Castle Douglas to Stranraer and Portpatrick, access being over the Glasgow & South Western from Dumfries. This had become joint property of the CR, G&SWR and the two English partners with a stake in this part of the Irish trade, the Midland and the London & North Western, in the 1880s, the two Scottish companies being left to share the working in a difficult partnership. The passenger traffic between the Portpatrick line and the south had always run via Annan and the G&SWR since the 'Lockerbie Agreement' of 1860, but freight was another matter and there were elaborate arrangements for the division of the freight between the CR and G&SWR routes. The LMS was able to simplify this and effectively the line west of Dumfries became part of the ex-G&SWR system. This at least was economy arising from the new grouping. The Lockerbie–Dumfries line retained some through working of carriages from Dumfries and Whithorn to and from Edinburgh, but its importance was reduced.

There were two points to the west of the mid-Lanarkshire coalfield where the CR and G&SWR lines met, at Muirkirk and between Strathaven and Darvel. The Muirkirk line had been a Caledonian Railway thrust towards Ayr, to which it had running powers, but Muirkirk was a fairly natural geographical frontier between the two, although through coaches were worked that way between Ayr and Edinburgh as long as the line west of Muirkirk remained open for passengers. The Strathaven–Darvel route had been built as a defence against intrusive proposals from the Duke of Portland and was unsuccessful from the start, the most remarkable thing about it being that it lasted until the outbreak of war in 1939.

To the south and west of Glasgow the CR had shared the south bank of the Clyde with the G&SWR, with joint lines to Paisley and via Barrhead to Kilmarnock. There was also a Caledonian line intruding deeply into G&SWR territory to reach Ardrossan and Irvine but, once clear of the Glasgow suburbs, with no significant intermediate traffic until it reached the coast. This had useful access to the harbour at Ardrossan, but not at Irvine, although its offshoot to Kilbirnie tapped the Glengarnock iron and steel traffic. Apart from the joint lines there was little contact between the CR and G&SWR systems, the latter being remarkably self-contained. Although the two companies had managed to agree a pooling of their steamer services, and got by when arranging their mutual interests in joint lines, relations between the two were not so much bad as absent. The LMS had some scope for eliminating duplication, but there was relatively little obvious opportunity for closer integration.

To the north the ex-CR traffic fed over a single route north of Larbert and Stirling, with an offshoot to Alloa. At Dunblane the route to Callander and Oban diverged. As far as

Callander this had something of the character of an outer suburban line, with services to Glasgow and Edinburgh, but west of Callander the line entered the Highlands, with the consequences of outstanding scenery but scarce local traffic. The Callander & Oban had remained independent until 1923, probably to avoid the threat of conceding running powers to the North British Railway had amalgamation been attempted. It was a single track line, with frequent crossing loops, and carried a substantial traffic, particularly in summer, meriting its own observation car, the *Maid of Morven*. In CR times it had for the most part been worked by locomotive classes built for the line, various designs of 'Oban Bogie'. Connections were made to quite extensive shipping services at Oban as well as steamers at some intermediate points and there were branches to Killin and Ballachulish.

The main line from Larbert continued to Perth, with largely agricultural local traffic, and featured a branch to Crieff from Gleneagles. At Crieff this branch was met by another coming directly from Perth and they shared similar traffic, both serving agricultural areas. The Gleneagles–Crieff line had some through workings to and from Glasgow and Edinburgh, some of them continuing westwards to Comrie and St. Fillans. Traffic diminished towards the west, and beyond St. Fillans the connection to the Callander & Oban at Balquhidder shared both the scenic beauty and the sparse intermediate traffic of the C&O. This stretch did not even merit a daily goods train, while the hopes of its becoming a through east–west route were never realised. Perth was a nodal point, entry from the south through Moncrieff Tunnel being shared with the North British from the start. The CR, HR and NBR shared the station, which was the scene of prolonged shunting, both of passenger and goods trains.

Dolphinton Junction, taken from the Carstairs coaling plant and looking eastwards. The line to the extreme right leads to Strawfrank Junction and the south, that to its left to Carstairs station, while ahead the straight line, with a train departing in the distance, is towards Edinburgh. The branch to the right in the middle of the picture leads to Dolphinton. The home signals from both Strawfrank and Carstairs No. 3 are unusual in that they give the junction indication but are not bracket signals, the upper arm reading to the left and the lower one to the right. (David Stirling's Collection)

Lesmahagow Junction in the heart of industrial Lanarkshire. Motherwell station is behind the photographer, the lines at the bottom centre leading to Hamilton and Ross Yard, while those at the extreme right are the main line south. The lines beyond the signal box to the right lead to Mossend, Coatbridge and the north, while those in the centre distance are to Glasgow. When the Caledonian Railway was opened in 1848, and for some time, main line trains ran via Coatbridge to Buchanan Street once that station opened, and so these lines were termed the main lines here, while the direct line was the 'Clydesdale line'. The direct line to Glasgow was not re-designated as the main line until the electrification in 1974.
(David Stirling's Collection)

McIntosh '55' Class 4 'Oban Bogie' No.14603 makes a sprited departure with an up train from Stirling. Once fully employed on the Oban line, by this time these locomotives were put on other duties and the mixed bag of rolling stock on this train suggests it is hardly a front line service. The engine is passing Stirling engine shed with its fairly typical rather primitive CR coaling facilities. Apart from the liveries, little has changed in this view from Caledonian days. (Rail Archive Stephenson)

The region between Perth and Aberdeen contains the city of Dundee along with several large towns, with the intermediate land having good agriculture, notable in parts for soft fruit growing. The main lines, Perth to Dundee and Aberdeen and the NBR Dundee–Aberdeen route (which was joint property as far as Arbroath and shared the CR tracks from Kinnaber Junction to Aberdeen), were linked by a network of local lines, all CR-owned other than the NBR Montrose–Bervie branch. The railway from Dundee to Arbroath had been a Caledonian line which became joint property in 1880, after which the NBR presence grew steadily, although the working was still shared at the grouping. Both companies had running powers over the other's lines in this area and the NB ran freight services to Brechin and Kirriemuir. The North British company's rights at Aberdeen were largely through its running powers over the CR and its neighbour to the north, the Great North of Scotland Railway, occasionally made difficulties for the NBR, requiring the situation to be clarified by an Act of Parliament in 1894. NB locomotives were stabled at the Caledonian shed at Ferryhill, not on GNSR property, an arrangement that survived the grouping; the grouping caused some realignment of loyalties in Aberdeen.

The most important area for the CR, however, was the central belt, roughly the diamond shape bounded by Dumbarton, Carstairs, Leith and Stirling. This produced the bulk of the CR's revenue, for it contained most of the industry and mineral wealth, not to mention the majority of the population. It also contained the North British Railway and, although the two met elsewhere, in the central belt they were inextricably bound up, with both of them serving the main traffic sources. One cannot consider one without the other, a relationship that became no simpler under the LMS and LNER.

From the passenger point of view the main routes in the central belt were from Glasgow and Edinburgh to Carstairs (and onwards to Carlisle), Glasgow and Motherwell northwards to Stirling, and the Glasgow–Edinburgh route via Shotts, along with the traffic between Edinburgh and Larbert using running powers over the NB. These were the main lines, with through services and fast trains as well as a local service. Longer-distance outer suburban services ran from Glasgow and Edinburgh to Lanark, Stirling and beyond. In the Clyde Valley there was a complex network of passenger routes, westwards from Glasgow on both sides of the Clyde (with steamer connections at Gourock and Wemyss Bay), underground on the north side of the city, with the Cathcart circle on the surface to the south, as well as a complicated network to Hamilton, Motherwell, Coatbridge and the like. Many of these lines had dense traffic, although in Glasgow and some of the larger towns the electric trams – Glasgow loved its trams – had done great damage to suburban railway traffic and they had ensured that the Paisley–Barrhead–Lyoncross Junction line, although built and equipped for passenger traffic, was never opened to passengers.

The underground lines through Glasgow Central Low Level provided an east–west route through Glasgow, with a loop to Maryhill, while eastwards it gave access to the main line at Rutherglen and to Coatbridge and Airdrie. These lines were busy but grimy through their limited ventilation. To the south east there were loops to Hamilton, with offshoots into the mid-Lanark coalfields, and Wishaw.

Edinburgh had its own suburban services, to Leith, Barnton and the Balerno loop. The Leith service was round-about and its extension to South Leith, though built, had never seen its intended passenger service. At the start of the LMS period these had respectable services, though not of the same intensity as the Glasgow suburban lines.

Between Edinburgh and the Clyde Valley towns lay bleakest Lanarkshire: Wilsontown, Fauldhouse and Shotts, all with passenger services, Wilsontown on its own branch, the others lying on the hilly Edinburgh–Glasgow line through Breich, which sometimes seemed as if the sign makers had got the first letter wrong.

The trunk lines carried freight as well as passenger traffic, of course, the main exception being the Edinburgh–Larbert route, which the Caledonian used more for passenger than freight traffic, as it could route the Edinburgh–Stirling freight via Mossend and thus keep mostly to its own tracks. Within the central belt it was mineral traffic which dominated the scene. At the time of the LMS takeover, most lines had ordinary freight, even the Glasgow Central low level line having a couple of through workings, but in this case there was a circular line round the north of Glasgow, from Dalmarnock to Balornock, Maryhill and thence over the Lanarkshire & Dunbartonshire line to the Clyde shipyards and the industrial Leven Valley beyond Dumbarton. This had a very short-lived passenger service but remained as a freight artery. Glasgow, of course, had a multitude of goods yards and private sidings, but also contained several important docks: General Terminus, Princes Dock and Stobcross within the city, and others such as Rothesay Dock and Greenock down river. In none of these cases was the CR the only railway user, and only Greenock came wholly into the LMS fold. To the east of Glasgow were various colliery branches and some quite lengthy freight-only systems, for example that from Newhouse to Bellside Junction (at Omoa station) with its offshoot to Salsburgh, and a clutch of lines in the Morningside area, some serving Coltness ironworks. Southwards into mid-Lanark the original lines through Larkhall East to Brocketsbrae were densely populated by collieries and then straggled into the hills past Coalburn to wild and dreich spots like Galawhistle and Spireslack, whence a line to Muirkirk had been built but never opened. Coal also appeared at a few points on the Muirkirk line. Further east, particularly around Benhar Junction, there were more colliery lines, but beyond that coal gave way to shale with its associated oil extraction industry. There was more coal to the north around Plean and Denny, and on the Kilsyth & Bonnybridge line.

Much of the coal was exported at the only significant port the Caledonian owned, Grangemouth. The CR owned the harbour and the branch railway to it, but access to that branch lay over the North British system in Falkirk, and that company had rights at Grangemouth; the Grangemouth branch was operated as a joint line. The NB was a significant user of the facilities at Grangemouth, with a share of the traffic not far short of the CR's own.

This brings us to the position of the Caledonian and North British Railways, a relationship which in many ways defined the two companies. They certainly competed, for to a great extent they served the same territory. They certainly had their outward differences, but they also had a great deal in common and their interests in connection with many external factors were identical. There had been some notable periods when the two companies competed very aggressively, but both realised the costs of this and the competition was reined in as much as they could manage. This is not the place to recount the detail, but a comprehensive 'peace agreement', largely confirming one that had been negotiated in 1891 but only partially implemented, was made in 1899 and extended in a

Methven station, one of the Caledonian Railway's less imposing stations. The branch from Methven Junction was short, and usually worked by a single train shuttling back and forward, with the odd trip to and from Perth interspersed. Facilities were so basic that no signalling was required here, but the branch engine shed is conspicuous. (David Stirling's collection)

Rosemount station on the Blairgowrie branch depicts a typical scene in agricultural Perthshire with the train still an important method of transport for rural communities. (Niall Ferguson's Collection)

very detailed pooling agreement in 1907. The pooling covered traffic between competitive points and the extent to which the two served the same area can be judged from the fact that about 44% of the combined traffic was pooled. That actually understates the common territory, as private sidings in towns which were served by both companies were not counted as being competitive unless both companies had access to the private siding, even though ordinary traffic from that town was considered competitive. The aims of the 1891 agreement had been to reduce "unremunerative passenger mileage to and from competitive points between the two companies and by rearranging the hours of trains, alternation or otherwise, making return tickets available by all routes of the companies to give the public the fullest benefit of the combined service". The two companies made extensive arrangements for accepting each other's tickets, and later for reducing duplicated services, so that generally speaking the public got a better service and the companies saved expense.

The 1907 pooling included freight services and had a great effect on the routeing of freight traffic. Some of the changes reduced costs, for the diversion of certain traffic from the 'natural' route also had the effect of balancing the flows of this kind of traffic in each direction through the exchange points between the two companies. The remaining partisan routeing of freight traffic involved unbalanced flows of traffic

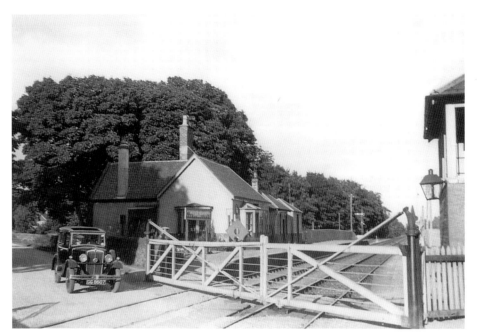

Clocksbriggs station on the main line north of Forfar, and served by locals towards Aberdeen and by the Forfar–Arbroath locals. The view is looking towards Aberdeen and is seen in the 1930s (the number plate on the vehicle was issued before 1932). The unequal length crossing gates are probably provided to take account of the skew crossing. Notice the lack of a footbridge, passengers using the footpath on the level crossing instead.
(Niall Ferguson's Collection)

through some of the exchange points, with costs which could have been reduced, although some of the more eccentric exchange points between the two, such as Camps and Dolphinton, were used much less. The companies did not tackle the question of minimising their joint costs by mutual use of their facilities and then division of the revenue in an agreed way. All of this, including the pooling agreement, was inherited by the LMS and LNER although after consultation the pre-grouping companies had given notice to terminate this agreement in 1932. They could, of course, have terminated it earlier by mutual agreement, but the looming end to this agreement was a spur to the new owners to put something in its place.

What else did the LMS inherit from the Caledonian? A line of 896 route miles, plus another 153 worked and 65 jointly owned or worked, about 43% of it single track, and a rather small amount (26 miles) quadruple. Its highest altitude was on the Leadhills & Wanlockhead line at 1,498 feet above sea level. It contained some significant tunnels, that at Greenock being the longest in Scotland, along with the Glasgow Central Low Level line, where the tunnels were generally below streets, and awkwardly sandwiched between the street and the water table of the Clyde. Permanent way was quoted as 90lb/yd bullhead rail, rather lighter than that of the LNWR. None of the line was electrified.

The Caledonian was noted for having some excellent stations, most of them arising in the twenty years or so before the 1914 war. Glasgow Central, of course, headed the list, considered by some to be the best laid out terminal station in the UK, but Stirling, Wemyss Bay and miscellaneous others, particularly those where James Miller had been architect, were

notable, although Miller's designs could also be seen on other Scottish railways. While this reputation for good stations was generally fair, the CR also had some awful specimens: Glasgow Buchanan Street reflected no credit on the company and it took the LMS to bring it to a level of adequacy, while some of the wayside stations, such as Brocketsbrae, Grangemouth, or Baldovan and Downfield, were poor.

Caledonian signalling was fit for purpose at the handover. The signalling at Glasgow Central was state of the art when installed in 1908 but by 1923 was dated, if very serviceable. Elsewhere, the single lines were equipped almost entirely with electric tablet working, most of the instruments relatively new, following a process of updating, while the double lines had the company's own version of Tyer's two-position block instrument, a design dating from the 1870s. A lock and block version of this was in use on the Glasgow Central low level lines. The Caledonian, like others, had considered updating its block working to a three-position instrument, and a few such instruments had been installed, but the work was not pursued. Nevertheless, the company had installed some track circuits in a gradual updating of facilities. Semaphore signals and lever frames were to the company's own design and manufacture.

Ancillary operations included extensive steamer working on the Clyde, on which there were six steamers, operated through the nominally separate Caledonian Steam Packet Company (CSPC). This was a substantial business, linking to the trains at Gourock and Wemyss Bay. The CR and G&SWR had pooled their Clyde Coast traffic in 1909, the NBR deciding to remain outside this arrangement, so some of the integration of the future LMS operations had already started. On Loch Lomond there were another six steamers, jointly owned with the North British, and smaller operations on Lochs Tay and Awe.

Other than Grangemouth the Caledonian-owned ports, Bowling and South Alloa, were minor affairs. Although it had been hugely developed later, Grangemouth had been inherited when the CR bought the Forth & Clyde Canal, which was still very much operational when the LMS took over. By then the other canal bequeathed to the LMS, the Monkland, from Glasgow to the Coatbridge area, was moribund. In addition the CR owned a number of piers on the Clyde and various lochs.

Finally, the CR had three hotels, all of them thriving, at Glasgow Central, Edinburgh and Gleneagles, and a share of the station hotel at Perth.

So that was what the LMS inherited. What did it do with it?

Economies of Scale

The amalgamation of three companies into one should normally result in some saving, usually covered in the phrase 'economies of scale'. The rather distinct territories of the three Scottish constituents somewhat limited the opportunities, but some economies were easy. The Caledonian engine shed at Dumfries was closed almost immediately and the work transferred to the more commodious and convenient Glasgow & South Western shed. The same was theoretically done at Kilmarnock, although since the Caledonian had essentially withdrawn from the Kilmarnock line in 1910 the shed had hardly been used since then. Matters at Carlisle took longer to arrange and on the closure of the former Maryport & Carlisle shed there late in 1924 G&SWR locomotives were moved to the ex-CR Kingmoor shed. There was less scope for similar economies elsewhere, for the ex-CR locomotive shed at Perth was far from fit to accept the extra work from the Highland shed, and at Muirkirk the CR engines had always been based in the G&SWR shed. Something might have been done sooner at Ardrossan, but that had to wait until 1931. In due course Perth CR shed was rebuilt and when that was complete in 1938, the ex-HR shed was closed.

The CR lines that penetrated into G&SWR territory, to Ardrossan and Glengarnock, had most of their traffic taken over by the G&SWR line, though the Caledonian line was necessary for overflow traffic and trains to Montgomerie pier until the war, and its western end was retained for access to the pier itself. There was parallel provision to Greenock, but the amount of traffic there could hardly have been handled by one of the two lines alone during the LMS era.

There was rationalisation of workshops, although it took some time. By 1926 it was agreed to close the CR

locomotive workshops at Perth and concentrate the work at St. Rollox, but within a few years St. Rollox ceased new production, the last batch of locomotives built there being some standard 4F 0-6-0s. By 1930 it had taken the heavy repair work for locomotives for the entire Northern Division, leaving Lochgorm and Kilmarnock to do only lighter repairs. The carriage and wagon work was removed from Inverness and concentrated on St.Rollox and Barassie. Although the CR had produced much of its own signalling material, and some of the CR signalling designs, such as the signal arms and lever frames, were perpetuated by the LMS, the ex-G&SWR works at Irvine became the Division's main signalling works.

Stations and Civil Engineering

The LMS inherited some fine stations from the CR and some others. Among these others was Glasgow Buchanan Street, adjacent to the CR's head office at 302 Buchanan Street. This in CR days was barely adequate, with four cramped platforms, a milk platform being available to form a fifth in times of need. The LMS rebuilt it in the summer of 1932, using the canopies from Ardrossan (CR) station, by then closed to passengers. A new wooden station building, with a small concourse, but nevertheless better than what had preceded it, fronted the station and became the public image of Buchanan Street station. It was then a slightly quaint, bucolic station in the middle of an industrial city, much better than the CR had left it but no great credit to the company. The LMS also made some improvements at Glasgow Central in the 1930s, where some extension of the main long-distance platforms, Nos.1, 2 and 11, was necessary because of the increased length of the overnight trains following the introduction of third class sleepers. There were few other significant improvements to the passenger stations, although the company did open a number of new stations – mostly halts – throughout its existence. Many of these were suburban stations and their description as halt merely indicates that the accommodation was basic rather than an absence of station staff, whereas the country halts had no staff. Appendix 1 lists the new stations. On the other hand, the company did little to improve the Glasgow Central low level lines, perhaps because they suffered badly from tramway competition. The arrangements for the King's visit to Clydebank in 1936 to inspect the *Queen Mary* tell their own story. The royal saloon was detached from the 'Night Scot' at Motherwell shortly after 9.00am, the station being closed to the public and other trains held outside for the duration. The 2-6-4T engine No.2418 then worked the royal party via Coatbridge, Robroyston and Maryhill, using the CR circular line to the north of Glasgow, long closed to passenger traffic, "to avoid the long succession of dingy tunnels" on the direct route through Central Low Level. Fare-

paying passengers were, of course, still expected to use the dingy tunnels on a daily basis, even if the King and Queen were to be spared them.

For a railway that prided itself on its locomotives and smart working, the Caledonian handed over to the LMS a decidedly mixed bag of engine sheds. Some, like Dundee and Kingmoor, were substantially built and well laid out, but others such as Polmadie and Perth were rather poor. The LMS made some considerable investment in these, Polmadie's wooden shed being replaced by a brick one in 1924-5, while Perth was rebuilt as a substantial place in 1937-8. There was progress too in such things as mechanical coaling plants, Polmadie receiving two during the LMS period, one in 1924-5 and again during the war in about 1942, while others appeared at Carstairs, Kingmoor, Perth and Oban from 1937. Mechanical ash disposal plants were another improvement by the LMS. The number of locomotive sheds decreased greatly under LMS management, partly through branch closures but more often simply by rationalisation where sheds with one or two engines were done away with and their work transferred to larger establishments; examples were Alyth, Blairgowrie, Callander, Dalmally and Peebles. There was a progressive need for larger turntables as longer locomotives appeared on the main lines, and they in turn displaced locomotives to branches. One odd incident, related by Jack W. Tyler, was the provision of a new turntable at Polmadie in the early 1930s, supplied by Cowans Sheldon of Carlisle. Cowans Sheldon installed a vacuum-driven engine to turn the table, instead of relying on manpower to do this, but the local Locomotive Department asked for it to be removed on the grounds that every depot would want one fitted. The equipment was then tried out on the LNER which let the proverbial cat out of the bag and vacuum tractors thereafter spread widely, including to the LMS. By 1936 they were well established and Stanier was praising their virtues in publicity material.

Bridge of Dun station, looking north. This shows the layout after simplification in 1935 when the north signal box was removed and the layout controlled from the south box, behind the photographer. Connections to the main line were rationalised, for in 1935 the direct connection from Brechin into the down main platform was removed, although it was still possible for a down main line train to arrive in the bay. (Ian Scrimgeour)

The Caledonian Railway had equipped its engines where necessary with large tenders and had managed as a consequence to achieve some quite long non-stop runs. It was normal, however, for many of its northbound services on the main line to Carlisle to take water at Beattock station if a stop was made to attach a pilot, and at the summit otherwise. The LMS, partly as a result of larger locomotives and heavier trains, took a different view and laid in water troughs at Floriston and Strawfrank (south of Carstairs) in 1927 to allow longer runs between station or water stops. When the official photograph of this was taken for news films the view, entitled 'The men who made the troughs', showed the Northern Division's Goods Manager, the Factor and the Solicitor!

The main line at Harthope was slightly realigned late in 1932 with a new viaduct where it crossed the main road, thus eliminating the effects of subsidence where the earlier alignment crossed the main road.

Permanent way work was improved by the LMS, the practice changing to supplying sleepers with the chairs already attached, rather than having to drill the sleepers and fix on the chairs on site. In order to achieve this the CR's creosoting plant at Greenhill was modernised in the late 1920s, thereafter supplying the whole of the Northern Division.

Kinnaber Junction, looking towards Aberdeen, with the North British line in the foreground. This was the northern extremity of the LNER towards Aberdeen, its trains suffering a 15mph speed limit over the junction. It was also an exchange point for freight to intermediate stations to Aberdeen not staffed by the NBR. Although staffed by the CR and LMS, this signal box was to a North British design. (Ian Scrimgeour)

Signalling

Caledonian signalling, as inherited by the LMS, was fit for purpose but not quite at the forefront of development: the current progress elsewhere was mainly in electrical developments of which the CR had few. Nevertheless, it had been keeping up to date in other ways and had carried out some economies in the early 1920s, with some singling together with the elimination of loops and signal boxes no longer required, and this continued into the early LMS period. The Northern Division also adopted the last design of Caledonian signal box, of which very few were actually built in CR days, as its pattern for new signal boxes. Examples appeared at miscellaneous places on the CR, such as Blackford, and also on the former G&SWR lines, but not on the Highland. During the war a few stray examples from south of the border appeared, such as that at Symington of an LMS design derived from LNWR practice. Wartime produced the functional ARP (air-raid protection) type, for example at Polmadie.

Economy was the pressing demand in the later 1920s as the economic downturn hit. Some small signal boxes were replaced by intermediate block signals, thus allowing line capacity to be maintained without boxes whose only function was to shorten the sections. Castlemilk, near Lockerbie, was dealt with in this way in 1933, for example. Some of the larger wayside stations had had signal boxes at both ends and

in several cases one of them was dispensed with and the other made to control the entire area. This usually required some simplification of layout and some motor-worked points and track circuits along with various electrical controls. The arrangements could be quite elaborate if circumstances warranted it. Partick North Junction was closed in this way (controlled from Partick East) in 1933, and one box each at Killin Junction and Bridge of Dun in 1935. In the same year at Lockerbie the erstwhile station box took over the functions of both the North and South boxes and a new box at Lanark Junction replaced three earlier ones at the vertices of the associated triangle where the Lanark branch met the main line.

Some economy was achieved by reducing double lines to single, for example between Guthrie Junction and Leysmill in 1936, and between Merryton Junction and Blackwood Junction in 1939-40, along with a handful of others, but very little of the former CR was treated in this way. A proposal to single the Alloa branch in the late 1930s was shelved.

The closure of Killin Junction West, and similar changes on single lines elsewhere, raised a difficulty in that the tablet for the single line section might need to be conveyed from the far end of the layout to a waiting train, causing some delay. For some years auxiliary instruments to alleviate this difficulty had been in use in connection with key token and

The west end of Princes Street station at Edinburgh in 1930. The bewildering array of signals was installed by the CR in 1893, and replaced by signals somewhat easier to understand by the LMS in 1937. The incoming signals have on each post two home arms and a 'precaution' signal, with a ringed fishtailed arm. There were two incoming lines between Dalry Junction and Princes Street, the upper arm applying to trains from one of these lines and the lower to the other; there were signals further out preventing trains moving towards this gantry until one or other of these had been cleared. This was at one time a common arrangement. The precaution signals survived longer on the CR than elsewhere, those at Glasgow Buchanan Street until the station closed. When the arm was 'off' it indicated that the platform was clear to the buffers, otherwise drivers could expect to find the line occupied.
(Ian Scrimgeour)

electric staff instruments, both on the LMS and elsewhere. The token was inserted by the signalman in his auxiliary instrument, which allowed the fireman to extract another from an auxiliary instrument near the starting signal, saving some walking. For tablet sections there was no really suitable instrument until the LMS Northern Division arranged for a new design to be manufactured in the mid-1930s. This was based on the Tyer's No.7 instrument, as used by the CR, but it could be produced in a version suitable for the No.6 instruments used elsewhere. It was used quite widely on the LMS in Scotland, and saved the cost of replacing the tablet

instruments which, in the majority of cases on the Caledonian section, were not very old. There was some replacement of older tablet instruments by more modern designs, usually Tyer's key token, which spread slowly across the system, and by isolated examples of the Railway Signal Company's key token instrument, a more elaborate and expensive design.

Other developments included a few examples of long section token working, although there was limited scope for that as the CR had installed the most obvious examples in the last few years of its life. The LMS favoured Railway Signal Company switching out apparatus, the majority of examples being found on the Highland section, but when Poniel Junction was made to switch this was the chosen equipment. In 1934-5 the Alyth and Kirriemuir branches received what was called 'alternate working' as an economy measure. Under normal circumstances these branches were then worked by a single train staff under 'one engine in steam' rules but the signalling at the terminus was retained, normally set at clear for trains into and out of the platform. The staff could be used to free the frame to shunt or to release a tablet in a special lock and revert to tablet working. This retained the opportunity to run a more intensive service on days of denser traffic, but required the intermediate ground siding frames to be adapted to be worked either by the staff or the tablet. There were two similar examples on the Highland section but not elsewhere. A slightly more adaptable way of doing this, using technology known at the time, would have been to use no-signalman token instruments, which saw very little use on the LMS. Little is not zero, however, and there were sections worked by no-

20

signalman instruments between Coalburn and Bankend after the box at the latter closed in 1942 and between Girvan and Turnberry on the ex-G&SWR lines. Another interesting and economical way of working appeared on the line to Brocketsbrae. This line had been double as far as Blackwood, with many collieries connected with it, most of them with a signal box. The line from Merryton Junction to Blackwood was singled in 1939 and 1940 but to cope with the freight serving the collieries the second track was retained between Merryton and Dalserf for goods traffic only. The passenger line was signalled with electric tablets but the goods line had more basic working, with a train staff only.

The railway's block working received a jolt in 1928 when, in the early hours of 25th October, the down 'Royal Highlander' ran into the rear of a failed goods train between Dinwoodie and Wamphray. The accident was caused by a signalman's error (the signalman at Wamphray had dozed off and on waking assumed that the goods had passed) but it did call attention to the question of the CR's provision of two-position block working, without controls to prevent this sort of lapse. Two-position block instruments had fallen out of favour after a bad accident at Coke Ovens on the Taff Vale Railway in

The interior of Lockerbie signal box in 1946. This had controlled the centre of the layout but when the south and north boxes closed in 1935 this one was adapted to control the entire layout. The lever frame shown is of the LMS pattern, based on a Midland Railway design, with the illuminated diagram showing the track occupation as detected by track circuits, as this box's visibility was heavily restricted by the abutment of the overbridge visible through the window. The outlying points were converted to motor operation. The two block instruments on the shelf to the signalman's right are of the Caledonian design. At the far end of the box are the tablet instruments: that to the right of the clock is the Tyer's No.7 type for the short section to Lochmaben, while to the left of the clock is the No.6 design for the long section to Dumfries. On either side of these are the auxiliary instruments, of the LMS Northern Division's pattern, installed to save time transferring the tablets between here and a train waiting at the starting signal. The instrument in the far left-hand corner controls the switching between long and short sections. Note that modernisation has replaced oil lighting by gas, but not electricity. (British Railways)

Carstairs from the top of the new coaling plant, about 1936. The then new locomotive shed is centre right, with the station partly visible behind it, the platform projecting to the left, with Carstairs No. 3 signal box visible on it. The S&T workshops, formerly the electricity works, are on the right, while the ash plant is to the left of the coaling area, with its large stock of loaded wagons and stockpiled coal. To the left of the station platform is the goods tranship shed and some staff housing. The view is looking towards Glasgow, with the main line south to the left and that to Edinburgh behind the photographer. (J. L. Stevenson collection)

Pickersgill 4-4-0 No.14481 at Perth on 18th June 1937 with the sand van for Perth North shed, then about to have its work taken over by a much-rebuilt and improved south (ex-CR) shed.. The van was presumably for transporting dried sand, which suggests one of the sheds lacked sand drying facilities. (H. C. Casserley)

1910, causing some companies (including the G&SWR) to replace them, or at least start installing some block controls. The Caledonian had done neither. The Dinwoodie accident report did not, however, criticise the block working. The LMS considered its block working at various times and in the late 1930s carried out a systematic programme of installing block controls on its main lines, including between Carlisle and Glasgow. This was aimed at addressing the main risks rather than every possibility, and at many places a track circuit was installed in the rear of the home signal, this being linked to the block instrument, placing it at TRAIN ON LINE if a train were standing at the home signal, it being the LMS's judgement that the highest risk arose from overlooking a train standing at the home signal. By 1947 berth track circuits, to detect a train standing at the home signal, and full controls, ensuring that the starting signal could not be cleared until LINE CLEAR had been obtained on the block, were in place at 110 locations between Carlisle and Glasgow/Edinburgh, while the replacement of the CR block by three-position instruments was in hand.

The LMS, like all the grouped companies other than the Great Western, adopted upper quadrant semaphore signals as the norm, and these appeared in Scotland from 1928 onwards. They had the advantage of some simplicity compared with lower quadrants. It appears, however, that the Northern Division continued to manufacture CR-pattern lower quadrant arms, presumably for replacements, and these appeared not just on ex-CR lines but also on the other sections. Three of the grouped companies, this time with the Southern as the odd man out, adopted tubular signal posts in 1935, but this change was at first ignored by the LMS Northern Division, which continued to install lattice post signals almost to the end of its existence.

Closer Working Arrangements with the LNER

The relationship with the erstwhile North British Railway determined much of what was commercially possible for the Caledonian section of the LMS. The two companies had been in significant competition for about half of their traffic and, although there had been agreements to reduce wasteful duplication, there was still considerable duplication. The pooling agreement between the CR and NBR expired at the end of January 1932 and was succeeded by a large-scale one between the LMS and LNER as a whole, which had other areas to deal with than just Scotland. As there was some urgency in continuing the CR-NBR pool, in practice the Scottish pooling arrangements were separate from the general ones. The wider pooling agreement came into effect between the LMS and LNER on 1st July 1932.

By 1932, however, traffic in many areas was not as healthy as it had once been and would not support two complementary services, so the LMS and LNER began regular meetings to obtain economies by 'closer working'. At that time the LNER was still working freight services using its running powers between Arbroath, Forfar and Kirriemuir and between Broomfield Junction and Brechin, with LNER staff at the stations mentioned. Both companies were shunting at sidings in places mutually served, in some cases for diminishing amounts of traffic. The CR and NBR had eliminated some of this sort of duplication earlier, for example the CR stopped working to Knightswood in Glasgow in 1916, exchanging the traffic to the NBR at Sighthill for onward working. Some further economies had been put in place by 1931, when more serious discussions began. Bothwell, Crianlarich and Dolphinton, for example, did not justify two station masters, so one company's station master looked after both stations, while there were shared arrangements for cartage at others.

Although this is not the place to provide an exhaustive list of these arrangements, a sample will give the flavour. The LNER left the LMS to work Hamilton Palace Colliery, which was served by a jointly owned branch. From

'812' Class 0-6-0 No.17676 on a permanent way train north of Perth. Despite being a group of men engaged in hard physical work, bare heads appear to have been unacceptable for the photograph! (Niall Ferguson's Collection)

2nd October 1932 the LMS ceased working goods traffic between Leith North, the docks and Seafield, withdrew from the Germiston branch at St. Rollox, from its Camelon and Roughcastle branches in Falkirk, and from working goods on the Dundee & Arbroath (except certain trainloads between Liff or Lochee and the harbour, which used a little of the D&A). Until then the LMS and LNER had provided equal shares of the passenger, freight, and shunting work on the D&A. In these cases the LNER continued to serve the area, and traffic was exchanged at the nearest convenient point. The LNER stopped working to Forfar and Kirriemuir and on the Whiteinch tramway on the same date; Broomfield to Brechin had been left to the LMS alone from the start of 1932. More substantially, the delivery of freight for the last few miles was simplified in the Falkirk area: the LNER worked the sidings between Larbert Junction and Grangemouth Junction for both, which meant that it began working the exchange freight over the Carmuirs triangle. The LMS handled the sidings on the Grangemouth branch: it and the CR before it had shunted Grangemouth docks for both companies since 1908. Shunting duties at Aberdeen were initially taken over by the LMS, but later transferred to the LNER. In 1933 the LNER ceased working to General Terminus in Glasgow, and handed the shunting at Stobcross to the LMS. That year the LMS also withdrew its staff from the LNER part of the old City of Glasgow Union Railway and stopped working freight over it, although it continued to work livestock to Bellgrove as it was so near the exchange point.

These arrangements were echoed elsewhere where possible, particularly in Lanarkshire, but it is a measure of how closely the NBR and CR overlapped that the scale was minuscule compared with the NBR-CR achievements. In all of this the companies calculated the net savings and the effect on the two companies' revenue and tried to achieve an equitable balance, although the pooling agreement reduced any loss to the company handing traffic to the other. Some of these arrangements were more difficult to carry out than others. Some of the economies arising from the LNER's withdrawal from Kirriemuir and Forfar were not realised: they expected the LNER's horse at both places to be redundant but the traffic kept the total need for carting horses constant. The LMS handover of the freight on the Dundee and Arbroath section saved some LMS staff, but the LNER needed additional men to compensate: this scheme in the event made no saving.

The changes in passenger working were gradual and as services evolved there was some reduction of duplication between the companies, although general growth in passenger services happened alongside this. (See Chapters 3 and 4 for passenger services.) Some economies were quite evident, however: Dundee West closed on Sundays from 1st January 1935 and the LMS traffic was worked into and out of Tay Bridge station. Arrangements at Montrose for sharing were delayed, but in 1934 the harbour haulage was rationalised while the CR station closed to passengers on 30th April, the LMS trains being diverted from Broomfield Junction into the LNER station. The cost of adapting Peebles NBR station to accept the trains of the CR line eliminated a scheme to concentrate all passenger traffic there.

One of the ways in which the two companies had protected their rights was by placing staff at the stations of the other. Its extent is sometimes surprising. The CR and NBR had rationalised, but not eliminated, this earlier. The LMS withdrew early from Jamestown (near Balloch) while the LNER staff at Brechin, Forfar and Kirriemuir, along with those on ex-G&SWR territory at Greenock, Paisley Canal and Port Glasgow, were all withdrawn in November 1932.

Granton to Glasgow fish specials had for some time been shared on the basis of one company taking the traffic for one year and the other for the following one. As the LNER route permitted higher train loads, the traffic was moved wholly to the LNER from the start of 1935. Even excursion traffic was regulated. The two companies agreed that Sunday excursions between Glasgow or Hamilton and Dundee or Aberdeen would be handled by the LMS only, and those between Edinburgh and Carlisle, Aberdeen and the former Highland section by the LNER. Advertised excursions to London were divided similarly, Glasgow and Perth to the LMS, Edinburgh, Dundee and Aberdeen to the LNER.

There were discussions about eliminating some of the duplicated ordinary passenger services and withdrawal of the Edinburgh–Aviemore–Keith through carriage was agreed in 1932, but the two companies considered it would be impolitic for the LMS, say, to stop working between Euston and Edinburgh, with the LNER making similar withdrawals. The public had to be educated gradually.

Ports

Grangemouth, as the only substantial port the CR had owned, was given due attention by the LMS from the start; six new lock gates were provided in 1925 and a new dredger, the *Carronwater*, replacing the 1880-built *Forth*, two years later. Like other LMS dredgers of the period *Carronwater* was built by Ferguson Bros. of Port Glasgow. Grangemouth had been a major coal exporting port, with about 2.8 million tons passing through in 1923, while machinery and the products of the iron and steel industry, along with fireclay bricks and light castings from local industry, were the other main exports. It imported iron ore, pig iron and scrap, principally for the Carron ironworks, as well a substantial amount of timber. Some of this timber had been used for pit props as well as imported sleepers for the creosoting plant at Greenhill. This trade had been shared by the Caledonian and North British Railways, the NBR having about 45% of the rail business, a relationship that continued under the new owners. When the LMS took over there was some oil importing, and a pipeline to refineries at Uphall; the oil trade increased as time passed, with regular imports from Iran (or Persia as it then was).

By the 1930s there was still substantial trade in iron ore and pig iron, but the coal trade had fallen considerably, never to recover. Grangemouth had, however, become Scotland's premier timber port and the oil industry was developing. The LMS modernised the plant, replacing some of the hydraulic cranes with faster electric luffing cranes to maintain the port's reputation for rapid dispatch. Some of this was in a programme announced in 1931 for a £200,000 investment in the facilities at Ayr, Troon and Grangemouth. These trends continued and by the end of the LMS era the oil industry was well established at Grangemouth, while further modernisation kept the port healthy. Its normal business was with Scandinavia, Germany, Holland, Belgium and France, as well as coastwise shipping to England.

LMS

3

Main Line Working

Foreign Affairs

The Caledonian Railway was a self-contained entity and, like any other pre-grouping railway, it was bounded by various frontier stations where it met other railways, and which were only semi-permeable. Traffic to and from other companies, 'foreign' traffic as opposed to 'local', involved through carriages on a scale which today would be regarded as rather restricted, while for many journeys between the Caledonian and its neighbours passengers had to change at Carlisle, Perth, Aberdeen or other junctions. The coming of the LMS changed some of this, for the Highland, Glasgow & South Western, London & North Western and Midland were now under the same management, and the artificial boundaries

created by change of ownership were, at least in principle, removed. After grouping there was greater through working between the former CR and LNWR, but only in a very limited way between the CR and the Midland. The territory served by the G&SWR was very self-contained, limiting the scope for a great deal of through working. The former Portpatrick & Wigtownshire Joint line, although worked by both CR and G&SWR before the grouping, was effectively worked thereafter as part of the G&SWR area, with a marginally reduced service to the former Caledonian lines, and it will hardly feature in what follows. The Highland had long had through passenger services to and from Glasgow by

'Royal Scot' 4-6-0 No.6106 Gordon Highlander *on an up express train at Carstairs. The locomotive has the later, larger type of smoke deflector (compare with the photo of No.6100 later in this chapter) and a tender with a better coal capacity than the small Midland type with which these l ocomotives were at first supplied. The layout at Carstairs was ingenious, and the opposite platform had a short inset in which a portion for Edinburgh could stand, clear of the main line. This is the case in the view as the road is clear for a train to arrive on the main line. In some cases the waiting coaches would be propelled on to a portion detached from a northbound train in the main platform and the assembly could depart for Edinburgh from the platform in which the coaches shown are standing.* (J. J. Cunningham)

A splendid portrait both of the driver and of a spotless 4-6-0 No.14752, the erstwhile Cardean, *at Edinburgh Princes Street, with an unidentified 'Dunalastair' in the background. The headlamps are for an express and the route indicator is for a train to Gourock or Balloch, so the next duty is probably the through Gourock train. No.14752 here is fitted with the vacuum brake and a proper coupling at the front, as opposed to the usual single link version. The shunt signals are of Stevens' type, common on the lowland Scottish railways, although the straight top to the external moving screen was a Caledonian feature. (There was also an internal moving screen to give a green light when the signal was 'off'.)* (J. J. Cunningham)

Stirling station with 'Dunalastair IV' No.14364 on an up train in the main line platform. The headlamps proclaim this to be an express train, which is supported by its inclusion of one of the Pullman cars. The leading vehicle is evidently for lesser mortals travelling shorter distances. Stirling was a place where the Caledonian, and the LMS after it, re-marshalled many trains, the Oban services often being split or combined here. Additional activity was provided by the LNER workings on the Forth and Clyde Junction line and the line to Alloa and Dunfermline, as well as the associated LNER trains over the LMS line to Greenhill.

(J. J. Cunningham)

the CR and Edinburgh by the North British, a pattern which continued after the grouping, but Perth remained a frontier station. As their territories overlapped so much there was little through passenger traffic between the former CR and NBR other than that worked by one or other of them under running powers, a situation which continued into the grouping with little change. Freight was broadly similar, although the grouped companies did make some significant efforts to economise here. The one area in which the grouping reduced what was on offer was the summer through Glasgow–Elgin passenger service which the CR had worked jointly with the

Great North of Scotland Railway, and which withered after the grouping, being replaced by through workings to the old NB section. A more distant memory was the through Glasgow–Newcastle services once operated by the CR and North Eastern Railway via Carlisle: the LNER had no interest in resurrecting these.

Passenger Working

By the time of the grouping the railways had partially recovered from the cuts imposed during the 1914-18 war, services being progressively restored in the following few years. To see the effects of the management of the LMS, as opposed to the legacy of the CR, we shall compare services in 1925, once things had settled down after the grouping, with those in 1938, the last year before war. The post-1945 railway was a much run-down and different affair. Before doing this we should notice the remarkable services offered in 1923, when the new grouped railways threw to the winds lessons their North British and Caledonian constituents had learned, and laid on duplicated through services. Both companies offered London–Lossiemouth sleepers (via Aberdeen), the traditional Glasgow–Elgin via Aberdeen and Dufftown summer train was supplemented by an Edinburgh–Elgin via Glenfarg and Aviemore one, along with other LNER through workings on to the GNSR. Both companies ran through carriages from Aberdeen to Penzance. (The return Penzance–Aberdeen working even appeared to be non-stop between Shrewsbury and Stirling, as it was attached to a mail train at Crewe and its stops were not advertised!) Glasgow had through carriages between Buchanan Street and Aberfeldy (twice a day in summer) and Loch Tay (once). Most of these were not to be repeated, although summer 1924 produced its own feature, with a through carriage in both directions between Gleneagles and London St. Pancras. Summer 1929 even saw one of the Sunday departures from Glasgow Central having a portion for St. Pancras.

Leaving aside various dated services, or those restricted to one day of the week, in 1925 Euston sent two daytime trains each with portions for Glasgow and Edinburgh, three to Aberdeen (but one of them arrived in the small hours of the morning, and was not an effective through passenger service), and another to Perth, while there was a further service from Birmingham and five from Liverpool or Manchester (or both) to Glasgow or Edinburgh (or both). In addition there were overnight services from London to Glasgow (three, one of them via Kilmarnock), Edinburgh (one), Aberdeen (two), Inverness (two) and a Lancashire–Glasgow/Edinburgh service. Oban had a through carriage and a sleeper service to and from Euston, but not its own train, while Dundee had through carriages on one day and sleepers

on one night train. Through carriages came from as far as Plymouth via the North & West line through Hereford to Glasgow.

By 1938 there was an extra day service from Euston to Glasgow running via Kilmarnock, but the same overnight provision as before, while Edinburgh's day services were reduced to just one train. Although the London–Perth provision had increased to two trains, with a third from Crewe, Aberdeen was reduced to two Euston services (one of them arriving at 3.00am) plus a sleeper. Dundee retained a sleeper but had no daytime services to Euston. The services from Birmingham and Lancashire were of the same quantity as in 1925, although one of these trains now had (separate) through carriages between Glasgow and both Blackpool and Southport, while another formed an overnight service from Halifax. The through carriages to and from the West Country now ran to Penzance. The net effect of this was some focussing of the LMS services on the western side of the country, leaving Edinburgh and Aberdeen more to the LNER. However, the big improvement over the period was the speeding up of the main services. Euston–Glasgow services were between an hour and half and two hours faster, with two of the three Perth services showing cuts of three quarters of an hour or more in the running time, with an hour or so cut from the Liverpool–Glasgow times. This, combined with the improved rolling stock, made a significant improvement in the quality of travel.

By 1938 summer holidays some distance from home were part of the social scene and the railways naturally adapted to cope with this. The summer Saturday trains showed some imagination, although some were slightly eccentric, such as the Liverpool–Larbert train, with a good onward connection to Oban and Dundee. Llandudno and Blackpool had trains to Edinburgh and Glasgow, while Halifax and Paignton had Glasgow services. Some of the Saturday services used unusual routes (eg Glasgow to Liverpool via Beattock, Hellifield and Manchester). It is interesting to note that there were services using other than the traditional routes: the Glasgow–Euston via Kilmarnock train mentioned, and summer Saturday trains over Beattock which ran to or from Sheffield or Manchester over the Settle & Carlisle. The grouping had evidently brought passengers some benefits.

There was less change in the internal Scottish provision and indeed there was less scope. The CR had run a good service of main line trains, with much exchange of through carriages at junctions giving a good range of through services, as well as branch line connections, and broadly speaking the LMS continued the practice. To the south of the central lowlands the main services were those to England, supplemented by a handful of local stopping services. The

'Tinto Express' provided a reasonably fast morning service from Moffat and Peebles to Glasgow and Edinburgh with an afternoon return. This evolved slightly over time, and latterly Lockerbie was included, although the Peebles passengers had to change trains. There were through Edinburgh–Dumfries and Whithorn workings over the Dumfries–Lockerbie line, which otherwise saw a purely local traffic of about seven trains a day.

The CR Glasgow–Edinburgh service was worked through Shotts over a less advantageous route than the main LNER Edinburgh and Glasgow line, but it nevertheless had seven or eight fast services each day, taking 65-70 minutes in 1925, along with much slower stopping trains. By 1938 the number of fast services had increased to thirteen, taking about the same time as before. Edinburgh enjoyed one through working to Gourock and, as it had for many years, two or three to Ayr via Muirkirk and Ochiltree. These last were a relic of some infighting over running powers and it seems that nobody had the heart to remove them; they lasted as long as the line west of Muirkirk. The more serious, and faster, Edinburgh–Ayr service had used the NB route before the grouping but by 1938 there was one via the CR instead.

To the north there were, in 1925, eight Glasgow–Aberdeen services, one of them overnight, and five to Dundee (as well as Dundee connections from other services). Oban had seven trains, mostly through workings from Glasgow and Edinburgh, but two came only from Stirling (though one of these carried the London sleeper). Most of these trains had Edinburgh connections, with through carriages on some from Edinburgh to Aberdeen or Dundee. There were four through Inverness services from Glasgow, one overnight, but the through carriages, daytime only, from Edinburgh came by the LNER route over the Forth Bridge, as they had in pre-grouping times. The 1938 services were similar but rather faster, with about an hour chopped off the Glasgow–Aberdeen times (The 'St. Mungo' did the run in three hours), but the Edinburgh–Dundee through carriages had gone.

The LMS was rather more imaginative with named trains than the Caledonian had been. The Caledonian had been limited to the 'Grampian Express', the 'Tinto Express' and latterly also the 'The Granite City' and 'Strathearn Express'. The LMS stopped the 'Grampian', 'Tinto' and 'Strathearn' but continued the other, adding a good selection of its own, mostly dating from the early 1930s. The 1938 list of named trains on ex-CR lines, which included a reinstated and slightly renamed 'Tinto' was:
'The Tinto', Lockerbie–Glasgow,
'The Royal Scot', Euston–Glasgow/ Edinburgh
'The Coronation Scot', 13.30 Euston–Glasgow (except Saturdays)
'Midday Scot' (two trains, one Euston–Glasgow, the other to Edinburgh, Saturdays only and slower than 'The Coronation Scot')
'The St Mungo', Glasgow–Aberdeen (except Saturdays)
'The Granite City', Glasgow–Aberdeen, Saturday, down direction only
'The Bon Accord', Glasgow–Aberdeen, (except Saturdays)
and for sleeper services:
'The Royal Highlander', Euston–Aberdeen and Inverness
'Night Scot' Euston–Glasgow.
Some of these titles include the word 'The', as timetables showed in the late 1930s, but the LMS was not wholly consistent about this. 'The Royal Scot', for example, started its existence without the definite article.

On 11th July 1927 the LNER began running the 'Flying Scotsman' non-stop between King's Cross and Edinburgh, generating a lot of useful publicity. The LMS retaliated by running 'The Royal Scot', a newly named

LMS Compound 4-4-0 No.900 in the up main platform at Symington on 1st August 1931. The layout at Symington was convenient for combining and separating trains as the shorter portion could be added to the front of the rest by shunting forward from the bay platform and various other moves were possible. This had the added advantage of giving the Peebles branch connections to some fast services, a benefit most branches missed. The use of Symington in this way continued to the end of the LMS period but declined slightly in favour of doing the combining and splitting at Carstairs. (H. C. Casserley)

At Edinburgh Princes Street on 27th April 1928, after the arrival of the non-stop 'Royal Scot' from Euston to Edinburgh behind Compound No.1054. The train was driven by Driver G. W. Langdale with Fireman A. Bassett who are two of the central figures among the other officials posing for the press. Note that the tender appears to be well loaded with coal despite the record run for a 4-4-0. This run, and the corresponding one to Glasgow, was arranged amid some secrecy, as they were intended to steal the thunder from the LNER's daily non-stop runs between London and Edinburgh. To do this it was essential that the new water troughs at Floriston were properly filled with water, which Jack Tyler was dispatched to oversee. He was greeted by a non-railwayman in Carlisle, who asked whether he was there in connection with the following day's non-stop run!
(T. & J. Barr Collection, Scottish Railway Preservation Society)

---

service, to Glasgow in 7 hours 57 minutes, arriving 18 minutes early, without a station stop south of Carlisle but with an engine change at Carnforth. The train was so early in Symington (13 minutes) that there was no locomotive for the Edinburgh portion, which had to wait a few minutes. The southern section was run by 'Claughton' Class No.5934 and a 'Precursor' as pilot, while two Midland Compounds Nos.907 and 908 did the honours between Carnforth and Glasgow. During the following winter the 'Royal Scot' was altered to run non-stop between Euston and Carlisle, changing engines at the locomotive sheds there; it continued to split or join at Symington as before.

1928 saw more spectacular events. The LNER again promised a non-stop 'Flying Scotsman' from 1st May, this being achieved by moving the Glasgow and Perth portions to the following train, although the timings were not accelerated. The LMS simply upstaged this on 27th April by running 'The Royal Scot' as two separate trains from Euston to Glasgow and Edinburgh, both non-stop.

The 1896 agreement between the East and West Coast routes not to run daytime trains between London and Edinburgh in less than 8¼ hours or night-time ones in under 7¾ hours was reconsidered in the late 1920s, but it was 1932 before it was altered. The two companies agreed to faster timings, the schedule of the 'Flying Scotsman' being cut by 25 minutes and that of the 'Royal Scot' to Glasgow by 20 minutes, with slightly less acceleration for its Edinburgh portion. The non-stop summer 'Flying Scotsman' did London–Edinburgh in 7½ hours, with the 'Royal Scot' reaching Glasgow in 7 hours 40 minutes. There were accelerations by other services too. The *Railway Magazine,* however, commented that despite this, the Carlisle–Glasgow timings were not yet up to what *Cardean* had regularly achieved.

In 1929, no doubt partly to upstage the LNER, the LMS ran a non-stop special from Glenboig to Euston, all 395½ miles, the journey taking two minutes under eight hours. This was the return working of a special from Euston for the Bussey Coal Company and was hauled by No.6127 *Novelty* driven by *Cardean's* former driver, David Gibson. In 1932 the LMS was claiming the longest all-year-round non-stop service, with the 'Night Scot', non-stop from Glasgow to Crewe, 243.3 miles.

The publicity battle over non-stop timings had little

On 25th October 1928, the down 'Royal Highlander' ran into the rear of a goods which had failed between Dinwoodie and Wamphray. This view, looking southwards, shows the debris at the start of the clearing up operations. Compound No.1176 was the train engine and had come to rest as shown, with its tender in the air behind it, beyond and partly on top of the train engine, rebuilt 'Dunalastair' No.14435, which had turned on its side, causing the compound and the first van to overtake. All four enginemen were killed, but fortunately no passengers, largely through the strength of the then new steel framed carriages. (T. & J. Barr Collection, Scottish Railway Preservation Society)

effect on income – indeed some of the 'high speed' services were very shaky financially, as A. J. Mullay has documented in detail. Nevertheless the general effort had the knock-on effect of smartening up a fair number of other services less in the publicity glare. The LMS and LNER continued to make much publicity of the acceleration of their Anglo-Scottish services, each spurring the other to greater efforts. In 1936 the 'Midday Scot' was accelerated in the May timetable, the Glasgow and Edinburgh portions splitting at Lockerbie in this case, while the summer version produced more spectacle, 'The Royal Scot' doing London–Glasgow in 7 hours 30 minutes although the 'Midday Scot' took ten minutes more, actually a slight slowing. There were accelerations on the Glasgow–Aberdeen run, with 'The Granite City' cutting the journey to 3 hours 12 minutes. Both the LMS and LNER retained fast schedules during the following winter, both routes managing a London–Edinburgh run in 7 hours 35 minutes.

In 1937 the sparks began to fly with the LNER's streamlined 'Coronation' running to Edinburgh in 6 hours. The LMS riposte was 'The Coronation Scot', with the first of three sets of coaches and one streamlined locomotive, No.6220 *Coronation,* appearing in May. In July 'The Coronation Scot' began running Euston–Glasgow in 6½ hours, stopping only at Carlisle. 'The Coronation Scot' was not the only improvement: 'The Royal Scot' was also accelerated, stopping in Carlisle station rather than at Kingmoor, there was an extra Lancashire–Glasgow and Edinburgh train, while the Glasgow–Aberdeen service now had two daily three-hour trains, with two stops (usually Perth and Stonehaven). There were further improvements, though not as spectacular, in 1938

when 'The Royal Scot', for example, had its time cut to 7 hours each way.

On 1st September 1939 the Ministry of Transport took over almost all of the railways in Britain and all the fast train services disappeared, almost literally overnight. An emergency timetable, undated, had been prepared; services were considerably reduced and slowed with the timetable of 11th September. In 1938 the LMS had run London–Glasgow in 6½ hours with 'The Coronation Scot'; by October 1939 the fastest run took 9 hours 35 minutes. It was the same story on the LNER: the 'Coronation' had reached Edinburgh from London in 6 hours in 1938: a year later the same journey took 9 hours 40 minutes. These cuts were partially restored early in 1940, when 'The Royal Scot' was speeded up to 6¾ hours between London and Glasgow, but the improvement did not

No.6100 Royal Scot *on the Aberdeen–Broad Street fish train at the south end of Carlisle station, probably in late 1934 when this locomotive was regularly rostered to work into Aberdeen on a passenger train and return on the fish. Notice the small smoke deflector in an early attempt to cure one of the problems this class experienced.*
(J. J. Cunningham)

last and there were further curtailments in February 1940. One odd effect of the war, commented on by the *Railway Magazine* at the time, was the improvement in the cleanliness of locomotives; on the both LMS and LNER the blue livery of the streamliners could be seen instead of just grime.

Streamlined 'Coronation' Class 4-6-2 No.6225 Duchess of Gloucester *on an up train at Symington on 12th July 1938. The leading vehicle is a West Coast Joint Stock full brake, while the rest of the visible train consists of Period II stock.* (J. L. Stevenson)

On-Train Catering

As explained in the rolling stock section, the CR had owned few catering vehicles and the catering provision on trains was correspondingly limited until the end of its existence, when the delivery of the Pullman cars allowed a considerable expansion. By summer 1924, when the CR vehicles were all in service, between Glasgow or Edinburgh and Carlisle there were eight catered services each way, with an additional up service from Carstairs, most using West Coast Joint Stock cars, but one in either direction used one of the CR Pullmans, although its northbound journey was on the sleeper from Carlisle to Glasgow Central via Kilmarnock. In addition there was a through West Coast restaurant car to and from Perth. On the rest of the former CR, there were seven services each way (six on Saturdays) between Glasgow and Edinburgh which had (Pullman) buffet cars, four Aberdeen services each way with restaurants and an additional one to Forfar which had no corresponding return, two between Perth and Carstairs or Symington (connecting with West Coast services), along with one buffet and the *Maid of Morven* buffet/observation car on the Oban line. In addition, there were three services between Perth and Aviemore or Inverness, one of them through to Glasgow, worked by ex-Caledonian catering vehicles. More interestingly there was a return working between Perth and Blair Atholl, to provide evening catering on a southbound sleeper. This was a noticeable amplification of what the CR had managed in its last days.

By 1938 the provision had enlarged, in part because the general level of long-distance services had increased. The Edinburgh–Glasgow catering service remained much as before while there was a slight increase in the provision between Edinburgh, Glasgow and Carlisle. Aberdeen had six catered services with two more between Glasgow and Perth, some of them through to the Highland section, while there were still three trains between Perth and the south which had catering. The big change, however, was on the Oban line, where five services had catering, mostly to or from Glasgow.

Sleeper Services

The Caledonian section of the LMS inherited sleeper services between Euston and Glasgow, Edinburgh, Dundee, Aberdeen, Inverness and Oban, along with Liverpool–Glasgow and an internal Scottish route between Glasgow and Inverness, the latter being essentially a Highland Railway legacy. At the beginning of the LMS period there were two sleeper trains between Euston and Glasgow, one of the down trains running to St. Enoch via Kilmarnock. This continued for many years, giving a sleeper service to the larger towns as far as

Kilmarnock. There was no corresponding service in the up direction. The Stranraer service ran via Annan mostly to Euston, but for a while to St. Pancras, the service in summer 1924 being on most nights from St. Pancras to Stranraer but returning from Stranraer to Euston. This eccentricity did not last long. There were competing sleepers on Anglo-Scottish services by the Midland and East Coast routes.

All of these sleeper services were first class only, as they had been since their introduction, third class passengers having to make do with ordinary seating on the overnight services. Third class sleeper services were introduced by the LMS, LNER and GWR, for the first time in the UK, on 24th September 1928. The LMS services ran between London and Aberdeen, Edinburgh, Glasgow, Inverness and Stranraer, the LNER doing much the same on the drier side of the country – to Newcastle, Edinburgh, Glasgow and Aberdeen. Oban had third class provision by 1929, although the Liverpool–Glasgow route remained first class only. Within a few years the remaining sleeper services carried both classes of passenger. Composite sleeping cars were introduced in 1930. Third class sleeper passengers were accommodated in convertible compartments, upper berths folding down from the compartment wall, with four berths to a compartment, each passenger being supplied with a rug and pillow: The fare supplement for Anglo-Scottish services was seven shillings. 'Ladies only' sleeping compartments were available on request. The third class sleepers were instantly popular; during the first fortnight 3,500 berths were booked. New sleeping cars, not convertible for daytime use, but otherwise similar to the earlier ones, were introduced in 1933.

In 1938 a sleeper service was introduced between Birmingham and Glasgow, the other routes remaining in operation, although Glasgow then had sleepers to both Manchester and Liverpool. The up Aberdeen sleeper detached a portion at Crewe which worked forward to Bletchley, with corresponding return sleepers from Bletchley to Aberdeen and Inverness and there was a Rugby to Glasgow service, leading to interesting speculation about the market for these. The sleeping coach services were quite extensive at this period at a time when, even with the accelerated streamlined trains, a return London–Glasgow or even Lancashire–Glasgow business trip in a day was scarcely possible, so using a sleeper in at least one direction made sense, while for others it saved most of a day spent in a train.

One effect of the war, apart from the drastic cutback in passenger services, was the withdrawal of third class sleepers on the LNER, and restriction on their use on the LMS. This led to the anomalous situation where for a time in 1940 the Edinburgh–Euston third class sleeper service used LNER stock on what was purely an LMS service.

Freight Working

We shall compare developments which took place between 1926 and 1938. Freight workings in pre-grouping times had been even more compartmentalised into individual companies than the passenger services, with virtually no freight trains scheduled to cross company borders other than by virtue of running powers or similar arrangements. Like many railways, the Caledonian worked trunk freights between main centres, to and from which there was much local trip working. There was little if any direct working between traffic sources and destinations without such intermediate remarshalling. The key centres were Carlisle, Carstairs, Edinburgh, Motherwell, Mossend, Gushetfaulds, Greenock, Buchanan Street/St. Rollox/Robroyston, Greenhill, Grangemouth, Stirling, Perth and Aberdeen. The Caledonian had used marshalling yards near most of these: Polmadie, Robroyston, Strathaven Junction, Ross Yard, Mossend, Fouldubs and Gorgie in particular, although of these only Robroyston and Ross used gravity to assist the marshalling, the others using locomotives. CR freight working was slightly dated.

By 1926 there was a slight dent in the territorial insularity of the ex-CR as there was by then a scheduled Ayr–Perth freight. That eliminated the delays of interchange in Glasgow at Shields Road between G&SWR and CR (or, worse, between G&SWR and NBR at Glasgow High Street then from NBR to the CR at Perth, which had been the usual G&SWR routeing, using its running powers to route freight to places on the former Scottish Central and Scottish North Eastern Railways via the North British).

A blow-by-blow account of the trunk services would be little more than a list of trains. The outline given will

CR 'River' Class 4-6-0 No.14759 on the down goods line at Carstairs with a freight. This was the main line through the station for freight traffic and the line to its left is a siding with, unusually, a set of wide to gauge trap points. To the left 4-4-0 'Dunalastair IV' Class No.14353 is on a semi-fast Glasgow train, having called at the platform inset to the left, probably to detach a portion for Edinburgh.
(J. J. Cunningham)

concentrate on the daily services; in many cases there were extras on certain days of the week. In the case of some of the services mentioned the balancing workings came from places close but not identical to the outward destinations, and it must be remembered that despite the beneficial effects of the wagon pooling system, there was still a great deal of working of empty wagons.

Carlisle had through freights to St. Rollox and Buchanan Street (5), Gushetfaulds (3), Edinburgh (Gorgie) (2), Perth (3), Mossend (2) and Aberdeen (1 plus a fish), with single services to Whifflet, Strathaven Junction (Hamilton), Motherwell, Strawfrank Junction (Carstairs), Stirling, Grangemouth, Dundee and Greenock, as well as some stopping freights. The main line to Carstairs had some workings northwards to and from Lockerbie but by the LMS period the CR freight route from Carlisle to Stranraer via Lockerbie had been eliminated in favour of the shorter Annan route. The Edinburgh line from Carstairs looked more of a branch from the freight perspective than it did for passenger services: there were the two Carlisle freights and a couple of milk trains, along with a couple of trains working part way to Wilsontown or Cobbinshaw from either end for the coal or

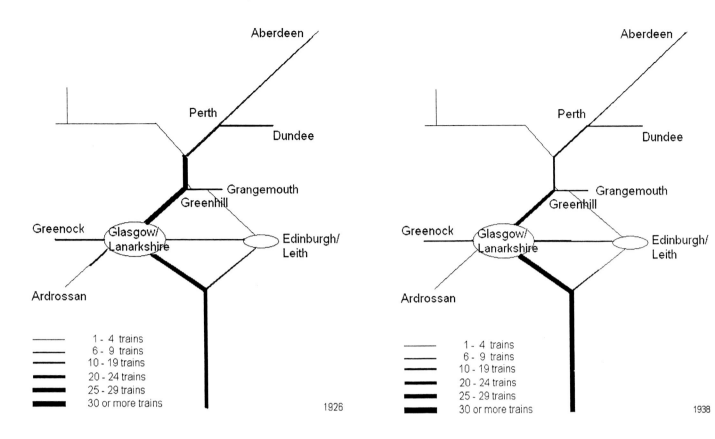

1 - 4 trains
6 - 9 trains
10 - 19 trains
20 - 24 trains
25 - 29 trains
30 or more trains

1926

1 - 4 trains
6 - 9 trains
10 - 19 trains
20 - 24 trains
25 - 29 trains
30 or more trains

1938

The density of scheduled freight trains in 1926 (left) and 1938 (right).

shale traffic. Leith and Granton had about half a dozen trains each, some of them short workings: the CR was not a big player at Leith.

Of course, the main line from Carstairs north west into the Clyde Valley carried the various through freights from Carlisle to Glasgow and the north, along with a couple of extra workings to and from Carstairs, but west of Law Junction there were many workings between the various traffic centres and any amount of trip working. It is easy to underestimate the freight on the CR's Glasgow–Edinburgh line: Buchanan Street sent two freights to Edinburgh with another four from destinations in the west and one from Grangemouth to the Edinburgh/Leith area, along with two or three, plus trip workings, to and from the Shotts–Addiewell–Oakbank areas from each end. The LMS continued to use the LNER line between Edinburgh and Larbert for freight but only very sparingly and mainly for overnight services, routeing other freights by the longer route via Mossend to keep mostly to LMS tracks.

The main line north was similar in concept, in that there were through freights from the main centres in the Clyde Valley and Carlisle, to Grangemouth, Stirling, Perth and Aberdeen. Stirling had about six such services, Perth slightly more and a few each to Dundee and Aberdeen. Forfar too featured, with through services from Edinburgh and Glasgow.

These centres all had further short-distance working to distribute the freight, considered along with the secondary services.

By 1938 there had been some significant changes. The actual services were, on the whole, much the same in frequency as in 1926, with much the same pattern of working between nodal points. The sketches below show that there was a slight reduction in frequency north of Glasgow and a slight increase to the south. There were slightly more through workings than before, for example between Scotstoun and Carlisle, while Edinburgh had additional workings to Carstairs. The traffic working to the Wilsontown and Shotts/ Benhar/Addiewell areas was much as before in pattern and frequency.

This description conceals some real advances. Many old wagons had been lubricated with grease, requiring frequent stops for inspection; the LMS promoted oil axle boxes and its faster freights required them. One of the most noticeable features was the increase in the number of classes of freight train, with the faster freights being required to have a proportion of the vehicles fitted with vacuum brakes and the rest piped for the vacuum brake. There were two types of fast freight. 'Fitted Freight No.1' was vacuum piped throughout, with at least 50% of the train brake-fitted and with screw or Instanter couplings; in addition, all vehicles had to have oil

34

Horwich Mogul No.2745 coasts into Lockerbie with a southbound freight in the late 1930s. The line to Dumfries curves off to the left and the North signal box once stood in the 'V' of the junction, by this time removed, control having been taken over by the former station signal box. Lockerbie engine shed, closed in 1931, stands on the right, although the place still merited a pilot engine at this time, supplied from Beattock. (J. J. Cunningham)

axle boxes and bolted springs. 'Fitted Freight No. 2' had to have one third of the vehicles at the head with operative vacuum brake, and had the same other requirements as above except that the rest of the train could be loose coupled. These trains were allowed to run faster then the usual loose-coupled unfitted train, partly because they could stop reliably, and were thus less liable to be shunted into refuge sidings frequently, and partly because the improved springing and axle boxes reduced the likelihood of derailment at higher speed. This not only allowed more rapid and reliable braking, but eliminated some of the stops to pin down individual wagon brakes before descending an incline. Some other freights were required to be marshalled with a 'fitted head', that is, a few vehicles at the front of the train on which the vacuum brake was operational. Trains with a fitted head of at least four vehicles were denoted in the working timetable by a Maltese Cross symbol and allowed a suitably faster schedule. Note that all this refers to vacuum brakes; the Westinghouse was steadily vanishing. The number of fitted freights trebled in the LMS's first ten years and significant accelerations were achieved in the early 1930s. By 1932 63% of general merchandise consignments reached their destination by the next day, a figure that rose to 69% by 1934.

The publicity wars with the other railways over non-stop runs even spread to freight workings. By 1932 there were two Aberdeen–London Broad Street workings, one for fish and the other for meat. The fish left Aberdeen around 9.45am and took just under 14 hours, averaging almost 40mph, including non-stop runs between Carlisle and Crewe, and between Crewe and Broad Street. The meat train was for Smithfield Market. These faster freights were able to run on lines with a good passenger service, without undue need to be shunted for the passenger trains to overtake. There was also a fast Glasgow Buchanan Street–St. Pancras freight about the same time, travelling at an average speed of 36 mph.

The LMS was an enthusiastic and successful proponent of containers, although the other railways also adopted them. Container freight really began in 1927, with the benefits of door-to-door service, reduced breakage and pilferage and reduced packing costs, all advantages that the road competition might offer. In 1927 the LMS had about 300 containers, a number which had grown to over 3,700 in 1933, despite the Depression, and to approximately 8,000 in 1938. There were several designs, the commonest being two ordinary closed containers, essentially small and large, with an even larger version for furniture, along with two types of insulated container, the larger with hooks specifically for meat, the smaller for either fish or meat, as traffic required, and three open containers, two for the sort of traffic typically using open wagons and a third for bricks and other building materials. This last one was quite small, and advertised as being capable of being lifted to wherever needed on a construction site.

LMS

Secondary and Branch Line Working

4

In addition to the main lines, the former Caledonian Railway had its share of secondary routes, such as that to Oban, as well as branch services. Some of the lines fell somewhere between those categories, being mainly branch lines but with some through working. For example Crieff and Comrie had some through passenger workings to and from Glasgow and Edinburgh, but the predominant service was that of a branch line.

Before the 1914-18 war the Glasgow, Barrhead & Kilmarnock line had seen local services provided by the joint line (although mostly worked by the G&SWR), a substantial G&SWR service and a few Caledonian Railway trains. Before the LMS took over the CR had given up the passenger working from Glasgow Central to Kilmarnock, the service henceforth being provided by the G&SWR from St. Enoch. The CR's East Kilbride trains continued to run into Central.

One feature the LMS attended to rapidly was the old Scottish railway companies' practice of charging a deposit on season tickets, refundable when the expired ticket was surrendered. This was stopped in November 1923, season ticket holders then being given the refund of their deposit when their ticket was next renewed.

Annan Shawhill station, with the single-coach branch train from Kirtlebridge disgorging a handful of passengers. The locomotive, 0-6-0 No.17101, was very much on home territory, having begun life as one of the locomotives supplied new to the Solway Junction Railway, as CR No.542, in 1868. It was rebuilt and modernised at St. Rollox in 1897, returning then to its old haunts. It was scrapped in 1927. (J. J. Cunningham)

'Dunalastair IV' No.14354 brings an up train into Kirtlebridge station in the 1920s, with the carriages still in pre-grouping livery. The Solway Junction line diverged behind the train, with a separate platform to the photographer's left. Kirtlebridge was served mainly by the stopping trains, although one or two semi-fasts stopped here to make a connection to or from Annan. (J. J. Cunningham)

Locharbriggs station on the Dumfries–Lockerbie line. This station had significant originating traffic from the nearby quarry as well as the usual intermediate traffic. There was a signal box and crossing loop, although only one passenger platform. It was unusual from a signalling point of view in that there were splitting distants governing the movement through the loop as well as the main line. At the beginning of the LMS period there were two or three substantial unadvertised trains for workmen daily between Dumfries and Locharbriggs as well as occasional goods workings between the two. (J. L. Smith/ The Lens of Sutton Collection, negative 51340)

Passenger Services

The glamour of main line services was only dimly reflected in the provision of local and stopping trains. In 1925, when the LMS was firmly established, between Carlisle and Carstairs there were on each stretch about five stopping services daily, mostly serving only part of the route, according to need. The Annan branch, all that remained of the Solway Junction line, had five services, one of which ran only when required to connect with a stopping service northwards for passengers travelling to intermediate stations between Kirtlebridge and Lockerbie (or Beattock in some timetables), returning empty to Annan. Passengers for Lockerbie or Beattock and beyond could catch the next train and use a later semi-fast from Kirtlebridge. Two of these Annan trains ran through to Lockerbie (but with no corresponding return). The Lockerbie–Dumfries service was healthier with seven trains one way and five back, plus a Saturday-only service. These were stopping trains but they carried through carriages, one between Edinburgh and Dumfries and another between Edinburgh and Whithorn, giving them some longer-distance traffic. Peebles was similar, with five trains and an extra on Saturday, plus the odd short working between Symington and Biggar, one of which included through carriages from Glasgow. Peebles, however, enjoyed through carriages to Glasgow in the morning (a 1¾-hour journey) and Edinburgh later in the day. In this respect the branches from Lockerbie and Symington had an advantage, for although the crack express trains might not stop, less exalted through trains did (and Symington had some services splitting or combining there). The Peebles–Glasgow services had a clear market, but those to Edinburgh were eclipsed by what the LNER could do with its more direct route. They were both vulnerable to the developing road transport.

Jumbo' 0-6-0 No.17440 at Biggar station in the 1930s. Although originally intended as freight engines, the later version built by McIntosh were fitted with the Westinghouse brake, allowing them to haul passenger trains as here at Biggar station on the Symington to Peebles branch. It looks as though two boys might have been offered an opportunity to get on the footplate!
(H. C. Casserley)

Lanark enjoyed a frequent local service to Carstairs, two of these trains each way forming through trains to or from Edinburgh, along with a dozen or so to or from Glasgow, the Glasgow trains in most cases having journey times of a little over the hour. Westwards the service was three trains daily to Muirkirk, with roughly the same in short workings to Douglas or Douglas West, most of these running through to Coalburn or Brocketsbrae, plus some workmen's trains between Muirkirk and Inches. Two, or in some other timetables three, of the Muirkirk trains were through Edinburgh–Ayr workings. This illustrates that Muirkirk's passenger traffic really faced westwards to Ayrshire and that the traffic on this line was dominated by the coalfields. North of this area lay the mid-Lanarkshire lines to Brocketsbrae and Coalburn, which had a good local service, with quite intricate variations of route. The Clyde Valley lines had an intensive service connecting Glasgow with Motherwell, Hamilton, Wishaw and Law Junction and connecting these places with some of the towns to the north, such as Holytown and Coatbridge. Some of these services ran through Glasgow Central Low Level. To the south Hamilton–Strathaven had about ten trains, three of them through to or from Glasgow, with some Saturday extras, but the line to the west to Darvel, which had reopened only days before the LMS came into existence, struggled on with four trains and the odd short working. The LMS did use that line for the occasional summer Saturday Hamilton–Ayr train, but there was little that could be done to develop it further.

The south side of Glasgow had very intensive passenger services to Cathcart and less so to Kirkhill in 1925. The southerly projection of the Cathcart line as the Lanarkshire & Ayrshire line had an outer suburban service of about nine trains at the Glasgow end, terminating at various places, mainly Whitecraigs or Neilston, but also at other stations as far as Lugton (joint line station, not the ex-CR one), with about seven additional workings to Ardrossan, one of them non-stop. Some timetables around that period also had a semi-fast commuter train. There were connections, but no through services, to Kilbirnie and Irvine. Gourock also had a good intensive service with about 25 trains daily; considerably fewer trains served Wemyss Bay.

To the north of the Clyde were the lines through Glasgow Central Low Level, mostly in serious competition with the LNER line and partly with Glasgow Corporation's own transport. Here again there were frequent services, terminating at various points as far afield as Airdrie and Balloch, with others to Bothwell and other destinations in the Clyde valley and one through train to Strathaven. Over the period there was a slight tendency for the LNER interest at Balloch to shrink. There were also less frequent suburban stopping trains between Buchanan Street, Coatbridge and points south of it, and a surprisingly prolific provision between Coatbridge and Glenboig.

The local and branch passenger services can be summarised as having either been improved by the LMS or

Newmains station on the Holytown–Morningside line, looking towards Morningside, probably after closure to passengers. The line on the right is one of the CR's access lines to the Coltness Iron Works, the main one being from Stirling Road on the Garriongill–Morningside line. The Coltness company was one of the main reasons for the building of the railways in this area. The distant signal visible on the right is for Coltness Iron Works signal box, where the right-hand line joined the North British access to the works; the NB line's bridge over the Newmains line can been seen through both openings of the road bridge. Newmains station had a signal box, behind the photographer, allowing direct access to the ironworks for trains from the collieries to the north, but other operations here were complicated by the steep gradients. The original passenger service to Morningside was from Garriongill Junction, but this was replaced by one on this line in 1864. Newmains Junction once lay a few hundred yards ahead, allowing a short-lived circular passenger service through Wishaw. Passenger services in the area were affected first by trams and later by the run-down of the Coltness ironworks, the station closing to passengers in 1930. This stretch of the line remained open to freight after the LMS period, the rest of the line northwards closing between 1930 and 1947.
(J. L. Smith/The Lens of Sutton Collection, negative 51412)

closed; in the case of Newhouse, both were done, and it had closed by 1938. The very intensive suburban services in the Clyde Valley were slightly speeded up, as were those over the Cathcart circle, while Gourock saw a significant increase in trains to over 40 daily. The low level services through Glasgow Central showed some polarisation, with evident decline in the service to Kelvinbridge and Airdrie (and closure beyond Airdrie to Newhouse) but a good service elsewhere. By 1938 Ardrossan had been left to the ex-G&SWR route, apart from the occasional boat connection to Montgomerie Pier, but the suburban services to Neilston and Uplawmoor had been increased significantly.

To the north of Glasgow the local service from Buchanan Street to Coatbridge and Hamilton shared the main line as far as Gartcosh with the services to Larbert and Stirling. There were about seven stopping services to Larbert, and four or five more between Glasgow and less distant points such as Cumbernauld. Denny had enjoyed a good branch service at the start of the LMS period, with even a through train or two from Glasgow, while the LMS and LNER shared the Larbert–Kilsyth provision. The LMS working to Kilsyth waned, and by 1938 both Denny's and Kilsyth's passenger services had gone. In contrast Alloa, shared about equally by LMS and LNER, saw a marginal increase in its service. In this case, however, the LMS had but one through train to Glasgow, while the LNER had several. The Grangemouth branch also remained in a similar position of being shared by LMS and LNER, with the LNER providing the through Glasgow trains and locals to Polmont, and the LMS the Grangemouth–Larbert trains. Camelon LNER station in Falkirk was served almost exclusively by these LMS Grangemouth–Larbert trains, hardly any LNER trains calling.

In Perthshire there was a good local service on the main Stirling–Perth line, one or two of these terminating at Gleneagles or running on to the branch there. Gleneagles to Crieff was served by a healthy thirteen trains each way, the direct Crieff–Perth line making do with fewer than half that number, although they were supplemented on Saturdays, particularly with some short workings to Methven. There was little difference in services between 1925 and 1938 despite the closure of the Methven branch – although the opening of

The Caledonian's suburban stations on the lines north of the Clyde westwards to Dumbarton were substantially built in a fairly heavy style, sometimes attractive, sometimes less so. This is Yoker station, rather optimistically advertising its serving of Renfrew by the Yoker to Renfrew ferry. This line served the shipyards on the north side of the river and shared a good traffic from the associated workmen with the trams. Freight supplying the shipyards with their raw materials was another staple of the line. (David Stirling's Collection)

Methven Junction as a public station and the working of some Saturday services terminating there mitigated any loss. The 1925 timetable featured a circular Glasgow–Crieff–Balquhidder–Glasgow working, not repeated in 1938, but by then there were frequent excursions in this area which did not feature in the timetable. Crieff started the period with two or three trains daily with through carriages to Glasgow and Edinburgh, more to Glasgow than to Edinburgh, and corresponding return workings, but by 1938 this had shrunk to one St. Fillans–Glasgow and one Glasgow–Crieff working.

Perth–Dundee was well provided with eighteen daily trains, along with four Saturday extras in 1925, slightly fewer than half of them stopping services, while the main line to Aberdeen was dominated by the fast or semi-fast trains, with three local trains making all or most of the journey, and additional local services at both ends. The Bankfoot line had quite a decent service, eight trains plus Saturday extras, with one daily train and three more Saturday ones through to Perth and back. Blairgowrie and Alyth had five or six through services to and from Dundee, with a couple of short workings on the branch to Alyth but another seven or eight between Blairgowrie and Coupar Angus. These lines also had the odd through train to or from Perth. The Dundee–Forfar line had a similar service, some of the trains having through carriages to Kirriemuir or Brechin, along with short workings to or from Barnhill, while Kirriemuir also had some through workings to Arbroath. The Brechin–Montrose service was interesting in that, although there were a few workings between Brechin and Bridge of Dun, or Dubton and Montrose, most of the connections were made by trains between Brechin and Montrose, these usually passing the service in the opposite direction on the main line between Bridge of Dun and Dubton.

Northbound main line trains stopped at Bridge of Dun to connect both to Brechin and Montrose, and southbound trains stopped at Dubton, again connecting both ways. This ingenious arrangement saved stopping the main line services twice.

Perth–Dundee saw some increase in provision between 1925 and 1938, Bankfoot closed, and the other services in the area maintained much the same service over the period, with the exception of that to Edzell which, although it had seven trains each way in 1938, was that summer only receiving an experimental revival of the service which had been withdrawn in 1931 and which would disappear once more at the end of summer 1938.

One general point in all the passenger services, particularly in the late 1930s, was the extent of the extra provision on Saturdays. For many offices Saturday was a half day, so the commuter services ran earlier than they did during the week, but there were additional trains for those seeking a half-day excursion, particularly to the Clyde and other leisure destinations. (These were the scheduled services; the LMS ran special half-day excursions too.) For many lines, including country branches, there were often one or two extra late night Saturday services to and from the main local town. In contrast to the railway at the end of the twentieth century, Saturday was a busier than normal day for passengers in the 1930s.

L. M. & S. R.
FOR CONDITIONS SEE NOTICES
Cheap Ticket at 3/4ths. Fare
DUNDEE (WEST) TO
PERTH (LMS)
Via Glencarse
THIRD CLASS   4300 (S)CT⁴/₃   FARE 2/4 C
PERTH
440   440

Sunday Trains

Sunday trains were a long-term issue for the Scottish railways. In the earliest days there had been the most strenuous opposition to running any Sunday trains at all, and most companies limited what they provided to mail trains and little more. The Caledonian Railway, while not serving an area where public opinion ran as strongly as it did further north, generally held to the prevailing opinions and ran little on a Sunday. At the beginning of the LMS period Sunday services consisted of roughly four trains between Carlisle and Glasgow, three on the Glasgow–Perth–Dundee route (with a single Edinburgh connection), and one between Perth and Aberdeen. Oban had its down overnight service, leaving Stirling shortly after midnight every morning except Monday: this might have been considered a Sunday train but it arrived so early in the morning that perhaps it did not count. There were but two Edinburgh–Glasgow trains. The only slight chinks in the dour Presbyterian armour were Sunday services to Gourock (4), Barnton (7) and Balerno (5), while Lanark enjoyed five trains, mostly Carstairs–Glasgow workings diverted via the county town.

Things changed in the inter-war period and by the summer of 1938 the main line Sunday services had expanded noticeably, typically by at least half, although considerably more between Glasgow and Perth, where there were now seven regular Sunday services. A stopping service southbound to Beattock and northbound from Lockerbie featured on the Carlisle main line, with a solitary train to and from Peebles,

A Drummond 'Jumbo', formerly CR No.331, in Edinburgh Princes Street station as No.17430 on a Barnton train consisting of then relatively new four-wheeled coaches. The indicator at the bottom of the chimney was a well-known CR feature at Glasgow Central, lasting into the British Railways era, but they were also used in Edinburgh, and from LMS times at St. Enoch. This locomotive shows the LMS management not only in the livery and renumbering but also the provision of vacuum brake in addition to the Westinghouse. (J. J. Cunningham)

but the Lanark service had gone. Glasgow–Edinburgh trains increased to five. There were, however, good services between Glasgow and Gourock (18), Wemyss Bay (8) and Balloch (13), while Edinburgh doubled its Barnton service compared with earlier years but, paradoxically, ceased providing services on the Balerno line. The Oban line now had the down mail running at a more civilised time on Sunday morning (7.15am from Glasgow) along with two trains each way for day excursion traffic, with few stops between Glasgow and Oban. A few other branches received services, such as Dundee–Blairgowrie (but not Alyth, Forfar or Brechin). The Sunday embargo had been well and truly breached on the routes from the cities, where people might spend Sunday relaxing.

Highland Railway 4-6-0 No.14686 Urquhart Castle pilots one of William Pickersgill's '191' Class 'Oban Bogies' on a passenger train in the up main platform at Connel Ferry on the Callander & Oban line. A short westbound train, probably a Dalmally local, stands in the down platform.
(Niall Ferguson's Collection)

A CR '191' Class 4-6-0, the last type of 'Oban Bogie' designed for the Callander & Oban line, running downhill into Connel Ferry with an Oban–Glasgow train. The earthworks visible to the right of the locomotive's smokebox were for a triangular junction, never completed, with the Ballachulish line. The train consists entirely of LMS-built carriages, the leading one being a brake third, diagram 1968. Built over a period of nearly ten years, there were some minor variations in detail as to positioning of ventilators and similar. Next comes a Diagram 1898 corridor composite with what appears to be another diagram 1968 example following. The last coach is too indistinct to identify. (J. J. Cunningham)

Drummond '171' Class 0-4-4T No.15103 is seen at Loch Tay on 28th July 1931. The coach adjacent to the locomotive is either a 45ft or 48ft long six-compartment brake third (they are hard to tell apart). In either case it was serving out its time on this very rural branch, as all the 45ft examples had gone by the following year, and the 48ft ones only lasted a further five years. The other coach is far more modern vehicle, a 50ft brake composite of 1910 vintage with side corridors providing lavatory access. All examples lasted into the 1950s. (H. C. Casserley)

A former Caledonian '439' Class 0-4-4T approaches Dundee West station with a short train. The leading two vehicles are both examples of the Caledonian built 65ft carriages known as the 'Grampian' stock, which were not uncommon in the Dundee area in the 1930s, with possibly a 48ft carriage bringing up the rear. This combination of vehicles makes it probable that the train has come from Blairgowrie over the Newtyle branch. (Niall Ferguson's Collection)

Excursion Traffic

The LMS was quite innovative in trying to attract new custom to its railways. There were many day and half-day excursion, some of them regular events, including frequent excursions to St. Fillans and the line through it, some pausing at St. Fillans, others not. These trains might form a circular tour, or simply run as an out and back operation. Bob Drummond noted in *The True Line* that on one day in September 1935 there were 24 excursion trains through St. Fillans, six each from Glasgow and Dundee, four from Edinburgh, and the rest from diverse places between Kilmarnock, Carluke and Aberdeen.

Oban was noted in the late 1920s as generally having three 'heavy' excursion trains each summer Sunday. In 1929 the company started to issue combined rail and dining tickets from Glasgow to Oban, valid on the 8.00am from Glasgow with lunch en route, and on the 3.00pm return working, with dinner on board. The fares were 32s (£1.60) first class and 16s third class, the differential suggesting that the meals for the first class passengers were considerably more lavish than those for the third class.

On 10th June 1931 the LNER ran an excursion from Glasgow to Staffa and Iona, the first to visit both islands in one day. It ran to and from Oban via Ardlui, doubled headed by ex-NBR 4-4-0 No.9695 and ex-GER 4-6-0 No.8502. The trip was repeated in July, but required only the 4-6-0 to haul it. These were repeated in 1933, all of this rather irritating to the inhabitants of Oban who were acutely aware that there was a shorter route to Glasgow than the one they were permitted to use. These excursions continued in similar vein in subsequent years, although in 1935, after damage at Ardoch Burn between Dunblane and Doune which caused the closure of the railway between those stations for a month, a few LMS excursions to Oban were worked via Ardlui. Other excursions where one company used the other's tracks included LNER circular tours from Aberdeen via Boat of Garten and Perth, or from Aberdeen to Dunfermline and Perth, outward by the LNER and back by the LMS route. By the late 1930s excursion provision had continued to develop, both the LMS and LNER offering circular tours between Edinburgh or Glasgow and Crianlarich outward by one company's route, returning by the other.

Sunday 5th April 1931 saw the movement down the Clyde of the new 42,000-ton liner *Empress of Britain,* which belonged to the Canadian Pacific Railway. The LMS advertised excursion fares to Langbank to see the liner, with three special trains laid on to carry the expected numbers. In the event 11,000 people turned up and another nine specials had to be hastily turned out. In those days Glasgow-bound trains had their tickets checked at Paisley, where there was only the normal Sunday staff, causing great delays and some bad press for the railway, showing that you can have too much of a good thing.

By the early 1930s, as well as day excursions in various forms, both the LMS and LNER in Scotland were promoting evening excursions. These were popular and well patronised, with a varied and interesting programme. An LMS innovation in 1934, was 'Whist Drive' trains on Saturdays. These used open stock and ran on various routes including a circular one through Crieff, the fare including a contribution to a prize for the winners of the whist drive.

The CR Ardrossan line saw significant excursion traffic in the late 1930s, as the ex-G&SWR route there was used to capacity and the CR line, although closed for normal passenger traffic, still remained in use for boat trains. Reports suggest that at the height of the excursion season there could be up to twenty passenger trains a day on the line.

THE "RUGGER" PULLMAN

Twice a year, between the hours of 10 and 11 a.m., Platform 2 of the Central Station, Glasgow, would be with difficulty recognised by one of its habitués. The popular 10 a.m. to Euston, with its large complement of business men and society leaders, is already threading through the "Uplands of the Lowlands". A strangely aristocratic set of coaches occupying the platform is the cynosure of all eyes, for on two Saturdays during each winter season, on the occasion of Scotland's Home "Rugger" Internationals, the now famous Glasgow to Edinburgh "Rugger" Pullman is run.

The beautiful *Marys* are there in all their splendour – *Mary Beaton, Mary Seaton,* and *Mary Carmichael,* together with *Flora Macdonald* and the lovely *Maid of Morven,* surely a good omen for a Scottish success. All seats in the luxurious cars have been reserved for days – the demand is greater than the supply.

As the hands of the clock approach 11, the platform and concourse are besieged by a crowd unique in the history of the Central Station.

Boys, wearing the caps of the well-known West of Scotland schools, rush exuberantly to and fro with as much noise as possible, as is the way of boys. Tall, broad-shouldered young fellows, whose names are household words from Anniesland to Goldenacre, appear sporting the colours of "Accies", G.H.S.F.P., or Gilmorehill. Immaculately tailored, ruddy-complexioned old fellows who talk of the glories of "West of Scotland" and "Edinburgh Accies" in the old days and bemoan the "decadent moderns", are well to the fore. And the ladies – fur-coated, silk-stockinged, shingled!

The passengers are ushered to their seats in the train by the smart Pullman attendants, and, the seduction of the comfortable arm chairs having been tested, the few moments prior to departure are given up to the greeting of old friends and a leisurely study of the "chic" souvenir luncheon menu cards.

"Rugger" is the sole topic of conversation. Will our forwards hold the opposing eight? How will we fare at the base of the scrum? Will Bannerman create a new Scottish record for the number of "caps" awarded? Will Murrayfield house the expected crowd comfortably or will the gates have to be closed?

At 10.59 a.m. the station master and guard have a last look over the magnificent train, and the whistle goes, regulators are opened, and with a hiss of escaping steam from the cylinders the powerful red engines get into their stride, and prompt to time the famous "Rugger" Pullman pull out on its 46-mile journey to the Scottish Capital.

And so to Murrayfield.

LMS Magazine, Vol. V, 1928 p169

Freight

The main line services worked the freight between the principal centres, leaving scheduled local and stopping freights to provide local service to and from individual stations, along with much trip working for the mineral traffic.

In 1926 the Lockerbie–Dumfries line had three daily freights, reflecting the line's use for access to Edinburgh and the north from Dumfries and beyond, along with an extra train between Dumfries and Locharbriggs, by then worked as a fill-in by a G&SWR section locomotive. Peebles had a single freight train, with a second between Symington and Biggar, while Dolphinton had just one, although one of the passenger trains worked mixed. The Muirkirk line had three freights to and from Muirkirk, with another from Ponfeigh to Motherwell. Trip working brought coal from Douglas Castle colliery (at Douglas West) to Alton Heights, along with coal from pits closer to Alton Heights itself. The Coalburn and Lesmahagow lines relied on extensive trip working to take the traffic to Ross Yard, whence scheduled freights took over, but the area was hard hit by the depression and retrenchment was fairly continuous over the LMS period.

The CR Ardrossan line had two workings, from Carmyle and from Polmadie, to Ardrossan and corresponding return workings, with some additional goods as far as Patterton, plus two mineral trains to and from Glengarnock. The Ardrossan and Glengarnock traffic was all competitive with the G&SWR lines, although until the war broke out it remained convenient to send some coal to Ardrossan harbour this way.

They way they once were. Class 2F 'Jumbo' 0-6-0 No.17360, a design originating with Drummond and perpetuated by his successors, on the Glasgow and Paisley Joint line shortly after the grouping, with what was then a fairly typical goods train. Notice the preponderance of open wagons, many of them sheeted, which had long been the preferred way of shipping most general freight. The move to covered vans came in the LMS period. The train is heading west on the four-track section of the joint line: the Caledonian had surprisingly little quadruple track of its own. (David Stirling's Collection)

Greenock showed its strong links to the CR by the range of destinations to which it sent through freights: Grangemouth, Gushetfaulds (2), Ross Yard, Glasgow College, Dalzell (east of Motherwell), Shawfield, Leith and Carlisle, this traffic being reinforced by one or two more from Paisley. There was far less freight on the opposite bank of the Clyde, with one Balloch service, another between Rothesay Dock and Wishaw, and three more from the Scotstoun-Partick area.

To the north Greenhill was a busy interchange point with the LNER, something the closer working agreements strengthened, and it also received and dispatched freight on the main line services. It had its own short workings to Denny, Alloa (2), Mungal Yard, Dalderse and Grahamston (the last three all in Falkirk, Mungal serving the Carron Company's line), while Larbert had freights to Banknock and Kilsyth over the Kilsyth & Bonnybridge Railway. The Grangemouth line had through LMS freights, and a slightly smaller number of LNER workings: the LNER remained an important provider at Grangemouth, being responsible for not much less than half the traffic.

Stirling was another LNER exchange point, but it also had twice daily freights to Oban, and a brace of local freights to Gleneagles and the Crieff line. Crieff itself had a further freight from St. Fillans to Blackford, and one on the direct line to Perth that started at Comrie on certain days, while Methven merited an independent freight to Perth. West of St. Fillans, there was no scheduled freight at all to Lochearnhead, with that station served from Balquhidder as required.

North of Perth, apart from the through Aberdeen and Forfar services from further south, there were three freight

workings from Perth itself, and others to Alyth and Blairgowrie, as well as shorter trips. Alyth and Forfar had their own direct services to Dundee, while Forfar had one to Dundee via Arbroath, and another to Montrose. Local services also worked to Aberdeen from Laurencekirk. In parallel to this the LNER still worked its twice-daily freights to Kirriemuir, and from Montrose to Brechin, the LMS running the same number between Brechin and Bridge of Dun, and four in all (one through from Forfar) between Dubton and Montrose. The CR lines in Angus and Kincardine were busy with freight!

By 1938 there was a slight reduction of freight services on some branches. While Muirkirk itself saw fewer Caledonian-section trains, the Carstairs–Muirkirk line was busier: there was a Carstairs–Auchinleck freight, a working to Inches (for Kennox Colliery), three to Ponfeigh and another to Douglas West, significantly more activity than in 1926, though one suspects there was less trip working.

Greenock's pattern in 1938 was similar to 1926 but reduced in frequency, while Ardrossan had little scheduled freight, for the Glengarnock traffic had gone to the G&SWR route, though some coal continued to run when required to Ardrossan. The line did see some interesting working, such as Newton to Kingmoor via Cathcart, Lugton and the G&SWR.

By 1938, however, the LMS had withdrawn from the Kilsyth and Bonnybridge line, but was otherwise serving much the same areas from Greenhill, except where workings had been swapped with the LNER; Falkirk Grahamston, for example, was handled by the LNER from Greenhill.

North of Stirling services were broadly the same as in 1926, with a slight diminution in frequency in a few cases. By then there were no LNER trains to Kirriemuir or Brechin.

Judging by the fact that the wagons have been repainted in LMS livery, this photo dates from some years after 1923. However, '812' Class 0-6-0 No.833 still displays Caledonian blue livery whilst shunting at Annan in 1926. The 30-ton bogie wagons seen had been the first attempt by the Caledonian to produce high capacity wagons in any quantity. The company eventually owned 400 examples but they were not a great success as the block trains they were intended to form proved too heavy for the locomotives in service at the time to haul in any great quantity, and such trains proved too long for the available goods loops.
(Niall Ferguson's Collection)

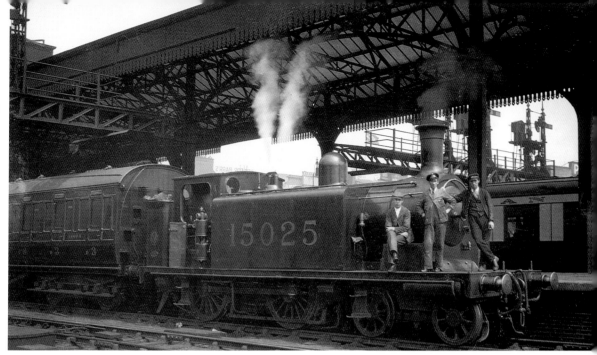

Lambie 4-4-0T No.15025 takes a break in its station pilot duties in Platform 10 at Glasgow Central, while the crew pose for the photographer; one of the Pullman cars sits in Platform 9. No.15025 was the last survivor of the class and had moved to Oban by 1937 where it worked out the rest of its days.
(J. J. Cunningham)

'Jumbo' 0-6-0 No.17396 at Oban on 9th September 1933 with the Pullman observation car Maid of Morven, *which had to be turned on the Oban turntable at the locomotive shed (some distance from the station) every time to ensure that the observation saloon was at the rear of the coach. As the Oban turntable was only 50ft in diameter,* Maid of Morven *was a tight fit and occasionally the curved panoramic window was broken during the operation. For that reason, certainly during Caledonian days at least, a spare window was kept at Oban and a foreman glazier travelled on the train in order to replace the window, should that prove necessary! There was some local interest in seeing through the large end windows just who was travelling in the* Maid *(the observation was not just in one direction!), but Hamilton Ellis's comments that "People rarely look their best when set behind glass like aquarium specimens!" had they been known, might have deterred some.*
(E. R. Morton, Niall Ferguson's Collection)

Leyland railbus No.29950. The styling may be of the 1930s, and it may have proper buffers, but the similarity between this and the 1950s British Railways railbuses is striking. These vehicles were based at Hamilton in the late 1930s, surviving there into British Railways ownership.
(J. L. Stevenson Collection)

New Ideas

The LMS did try some innovations which looked at the time to be promising, both from the point of view of economy and for developing traffic. In the summer of 1927 Sentinel-Cammell railcars made their first appearance on the Airdrie–Newhouse line, then in the autumn two were on the Newhouse service, one each between Perth and Methven, on the Dalmellington branch and between Hamilton–Strathaven, with yet another working to Holytown and Coatbridge. This was in a determined effort to bolster the difficulties being experienced through competition. In 1925 the service from Airdrie to Newhouse consisted of eight trains with six extras on Saturdays. By 1929, with the steam railcars, the service to Newhouse had shot up to thirteen trains with seven more on Saturdays, as well as seventeen additional short workings to Chapelhall during the week and an amazing 36 extra on Saturdays. That is, between Airdrie and Chapelhall there were 73 trains each way on Saturdays! The LMS was trying hard. It was, however, all to no avail and the line closed to passengers on 1st December 1930. In that year there were thirteen of these Sentinel-Cammell railcars, all in the Northern Division, where they were then joined by a geared version. The steam railcar was an attempt to retain traffic but the cars turned out to be less attractive than expected, partly through the dirt associated with servicing the steam engine, while their limited capacity could also be a problem.

The LMS dabbled with dieselisation and tried a few experimental diesel railcars, not all in Scotland. Three 1934-built four-wheeled Leyland railcars migrated to the Hamilton area, where they worked on various services, for example to Brocketsbrae and mid-Lanarkshire generally. In 1938, for example, one of these cars worked the following trains, Mondays-Fridays only, with a steam train being used for the heavier traffic on Saturdays:

> 6.45am Hamilton–Brocketsbrae and return
> 8.14am Hamilton–Douglas West–Lanark and return
> 12.18pm Hamilton–Brocketsbrae–Alton Heights–Lesmahagow–Hamilton
> 4.04 pm Hamilton–Brocketsbrae and return

On Thursdays the car ran empty to Stonehouse, and thence passenger to Lesmahagow and back to Hamilton. This car gave what must have been a very rare passenger working between Brocketsbrae and Lesmahagow. There was another diesel duty from Hamilton, working local services to Holytown or once a day through to Law Junction via Holytown and to Strathaven (via Quarter). In this diagram the diesel did work on Saturdays, but with a different mix of duties from the weekday roster, so the diesels were being deployed on the more lightly used services, leaving the busy trains locomotive-hauled. These railcars survived for some time at Hamilton, still being there at the end of the LMS's existence. They might have been more successful in some ways than the Sentinel-Cammell cars, although they also had limited capacity, but perhaps fingers had been burned by the latter, for it seems not as much confidence was invested in the diesels. **LMS**

5

Locomotives and Rolling Stock

In 1923 the LMS in Scotland found itself with an array of locomotives acquired from the various companies from which it was formed. Although locomotives designed by the Drummond brothers featured in the stock lists of all three companies, the Glasgow & South Western Railway was very much the outsider, as Peter Drummond had produced a limited number of locomotive designs during his time there. Prior to that he had, of course, been Locomotive Superintendent of the Highland Railway, where he had produced a number of successful 4-4-0 and 0-6-0 designs, but that company, like the G&SWR, was of small size compared with the Caledonian and, not perhaps surprisingly, prior to the production of LMS standard classes, the locomotives of the Caledonian Railway came to dominate the rails of the LMS north of Carlisle.

However, some classes were still quite small in number in comparison with similar types from the other LMS constituent companies, and also differed from mainstream LMS practice. Caledonian 4-6-0s had never been particularly successful, as they suffered from limited grate size and poor steaming. They also consisted of a number of numerically small classes, two of which, the '956' and '191' Classes of William Pickersgill, had three cylinders, adding to their complication and probably delivering poor performances through the men's unfamiliarity with valve setting (see below). Almost all the 4-6-0 classes had disappeared by the 1930s, with the occasional example lingering on through the Second World War. The only major exception to the elimination of the Caledonian 4-6-0 classes was Pickersgill's outside-cylindered '60' Class. An example of that class, as well as one of Pickersgill's 4-4-0s, was included in the Settle & Carlisle line locomotive trials of 1924 and 1926 and, as a result of its performance there, J. G. Barr persuaded the LMS to produce a further twenty examples, one of which was tested over the Preston to Carlisle line in June 1926. Following that, the new locomotives joined the 'River' Class 4-6-0s (see below) in working heavy freight traffic between Aberdeen and Carlisle.

Although locomotives tended to be repainted in LMS livery at an early date, that did not always happen. Class '66' 4-4-0 carrying the Caledonian duplicate number 1081 and still in blue livery (if a little faded) is seen at Forfar mpd in 1930! (G. A. Coltas)

The traditional Scottish goods locomotive was once the 0-4-2 and all the lowland railways had many of them. Brittain's CR design was one of the most attractive, of which No.17013 is seen here. Thirty of these were built, twenty surviving to the LMS, but they had all gone by 1932. The locomotive is at Dalry Road shed in Edinburgh, with the coaling stage behind supplied by one of the CR's 30-ton former mineral wagons. These were not a success, for reasons such as the poor availability of refuge sidings long enough for the trains or customers' sidings capable of handling the large wagons so they were diverted to serve for locomotive coal. (J. J. Cunningham)

Brittain '670' Class 0-4-2 No.17007, along with the 4-4-0 'Oban Bogie', the only two locomotive designs of that Locomotive Superintendent to reach the LMS, seen at Dundee. (Collection of the late Peter James)

The class lasted into the early British Railways era, the LMS-built examples being differentiated from their Caledonian forebears by the lack of inset sides at the front of the tender.

The 'Wemyss Bay Tanks' should be considered next, being essentially a tank version of the Class '60' with smaller 5ft 9in driving wheels and a 4-6-2 wheel arrangement. Intended to haul commuter and excursion trains in connection with the Clyde Coast steamers (as had the less successful 4-6-4T of the G&SWR, and whence came their soubriquet) these powerful locomotives all lasted into nationalisation, most ending their days providing banking assistance at Beattock on the West Coast Main Line, as even they proved unequal to the increasingly heavy trains of the late 1920s. In 1927 the first of the LMS 4P 2-6-4Ts appeared from Derby, construction continuing until 1934, and that class was followed in 1930 by the 3P 2-6-2T. Seventy examples of the 2-6-2T had appeared by the time William Stanier took over as Locomotive Superintendent, and he continued construction of the type, although with redesigned cylinders and long-travel valve gear. Ten examples of Stanier's 2-6-2T reached Scotland soon after construction began and were employed on the Glasgow Low Level lines, where they took over from the Caledonian 0-4-4Ts which, although economical, lacked the power needed to cope with increasingly heavy traffic on busy suburban routes.

Brittain, McIntosh and Pickersgill each designed a class of passenger locomotive especially for use on the Callander & Oban line. An example of Brittain's 4-4-0 design is seen as LMS No.14100. (Collection of the late Peter James)

'34' Class 2-6-0 No.17801 at St. Rollox. One of only two designs of inside-cylinder 2-6-0 to see service in the UK, withdrawal commenced in 1935 and all had gone by 1937. (Collection of the late Peter James)

'Killin Pug' No.15001 at Inverness in its final years before withdrawal. Note the various versions of the letters LMS on the saddle tank. Despite there being but two examples of this class, the fact that they were Westinghouse-fitted seems to have ensured the survival of this example considerably beyond its expected lifespan. (Niall Ferguson's Collection)

The inappropriateness of using former Caledonian 0-4-4Ts during the 1930s was not just restricted to the busy suburban routes as, on rural branch lines, they were under-used and too expensive. The LMS therefore decided to mimic the activities of some of its predecessors by using combined carriages and locomotives in a further effort to reduce costs. Of the LMS constituent companies in Scotland, only the G&SWR had actually used railcars, but the Caledonian had considered their use and had even reached the stage of commissioning a design in 1906. Although there is no evidence that the design was actually built (and certainly one never entered service), there remains the tantalising possibility that construction actually started, as a railmotor features in the returns of rolling stock made to the Board of Trade every half-year between 1906 and 1913 (after which date the categories of vehicle become much less detailed).

LNWR railmotor No.29988 at St. Rollox Works. This vehicle spent much of its life working on the Moffat branch. (J. L. Stevenson)

To return to the LMS, initially the use of railmotors was limited to moving one of those built by the LNWR to the Moffat branch. However, in July 1927 significant numbers of railmotors began to appear on LMS lines in Scotland, the first example entering service on the Airdrie-Newhouse line at that date. They were constructed by the Sentinel Company, who also built similar, but not identical, cars for the LNER. By the end of 1932 nine examples were in service on former Caledonian lines (as well as a further four on the G&SWR Section) Of these, one started work at Methven, near Perth, in 1931, another at Airdrie, two each at Motherwell and Grangemouth, and no fewer than three at Hamilton. The reason behind this distribution was probably that the railcars had only third class accommodation, and were therefore only considered appropriate for industrial areas, where their passengers would usually be workmen. Another was to be found on the Leadhills branch in 1936, but by the time that branch closed, at the end of 1938, it had been supplanted by

the gate-fitted coaches which had formerly worked the Garstang & Knott End line in Lancashire, hauled by a Caledonian 0-4-4T.

Unlike the LNWR example, which stayed on the Moffat branch until about 1948, most of the Sentinel vehicles had been withdrawn by the end of 1935, surely one of the shortest life spans for a class of railway vehicle ever, although one of the Hamilton vehicles did last until 1937, and another one until 1939. The demise of the Sentinel railcars may not have been unconnected with the introduction by the LMS of Leyland diesel hydraulic railcars. In June 1934 three such four-wheeled vehicles were delivered to the company, having been tested between Euston and Watford in February of that year.. They were 38ft long with 40 seats in two saloons, one each side of the central entrance, and one was tried out in the spring of 1935 around the Hamilton and Airdrie areas. After returning briefly to work in England, they all moved permanently back to Hamilton, the other two following later. From Hamilton, as with the earlier Sentinel vehicles, they were scheduled on short distance passenger services to places such as Coalburn and Holytown. However, as was also the case with the Sentinels, they had to be replaced by ordinary trains on busy days as their accommodation was so limited, and could not be supplemented by adding carriages. They were, apparently, unpopular and frequently broke down, possibly because the shed staff were more used to servicing steam locomotives. Although they remained at Hamilton until the end of the LMS era, they did not long survive nationalisation, and by July 1949 only one was in service, the other two being discarded at Hamilton shed: by 1950 all were at St. Rollox awaiting scrapping.

To return to main line services, the demise of the majority of McIntosh's 4-6-0s might have been expected, but the end of the Pickersgill '956' and '191' Classes came as a surprise to many. Despite their small numbers, the engines were of modern appearance, but were thought to be expensive to operate and maintain, and were considered poor performers by their crews. The late Duncan Burton, who ended his working life as Shed Superintendent at Haymarket Motive Power Depot (mpd) in Edinburgh, and who was highly experienced in the workings of the mechanically similar LNER V2 2-6-2s, considered that poor opinion to have resulted from a lack of understanding on the part of Caledonian staff of how to 'set up' three-cylinder engines, and that both classes could have proved themselves worthwhile locomotives in other hands.

At the other extreme, some locomotives which one might have expected to have disappeared rapidly managed to find a niche occupation where they provided service for some years. A prime example of that was one of the two 0-4-2ST 'Killin Tanks'. Originally designed by Dugald Drummond for use on the Killin to Loch Tay branch, which they worked week

Pickersgill 4-4-0 No.14490 storms out of Aberdeen in the early days of the grouping. Behind the leading fish truck, the first carriage is a 45ft third class carriage of Diagram 32 with six compartments and six lavatories (two between each pair of compartments) which provided facilities for all the passengers without the need for side corridors. Next is a 45ft Diagram 28 or 29 (it is hard to distinguish them) composite with a coupé end leading with a side corridor providing lavatory access for the first class passengers, whilst the two third class compartments at the far end have no lavatory facilities available. Beyond that is another Diagram 32 lavatory third with an eight-compartment 45ft third of Diagram 33 beyond that, whilst bringing up the rear is possibly one of the two 42ft West Coast Joint Stock (WCJS) postal brake vans which the Caledonian Railway acquired in March 1910 and which were finally withdrawn in 1923.
(Niall Ferguson's Collection)

and week about, the other example being stabled at Stirling, they were essentially extended versions of the 0-4-0ST or 'Wee Pug' used as a shunting locomotive all over the Caledonian system. Superseded on the Loch Tay branch by Drummond's '171' Class 0-4-4T, one was soon scrapped, but the other moved to Dumbarton, where until 1932 it provided a regular service at the United Turkey Red factory in the Vale of Leven (which required a short wheelbase Westinghouse-fitted locomotive to shunt fitted vans containing cloth) before finally departing for a period at Inverness depot before

scrapping. Towards the end of 1935 it was noted working the Dornoch branch.

Mention must also be made of three classes of Highland Railway 4-6-0s. Most famous (or infamous) of these were the six 'Rivers' designed by F. G. Smith. The first was delivered in September 1915 when it was declared that, at six tons more than its design weight of 66 tons, it was too heavy for the line and the entire class was banned. The Caledonian Railway, faced with serious motive power problems, leapt at the chance to purchase modern locomotives and acquired all six. In the early years of the LMS they were still banned from the Highland Section, but in 1927 the LMS Bridge Stress Committee carried out trials between Perth and Inverness on Sundays. That resulted in minor strengthening of the bridge over the Tay at Dalguise, and of a few culverts, following which the 'Rivers' were allowed to work north from Perth, although they were still to be found further south as well. Without the advent of the Second World War they would all have gone by the middle of 1940, but the need for considerable locomotive power to work troop trains on the Glasgow & South Western Section meant that No.14758 (which was still in service) was tidied up at St. Rollox and No.14760 was even recovered from the scrap line and returned to service. The two locomotives soldiered on during 1941 taking leave trains of fifteen coaches up the 1 in 57 gradient between New Luce and Glenwhilly. Both engines were in very poor condition and had to be worked in full gear. As a result their performance was truly awful, taking 105 minutes for the 38 miles between Girvan and Stranraer, even though double-headed, against the

Drummond '80' Class 4-4-0 No.14113 in early LMS red livery shunting matching ex-Caledonian coaches in the carriage sidings at the north end of Stirling station. These locomotives, with smaller driving wheels than the earlier and more numerous '66' Class, were built at St. Rollox in 1888–91 for the Clyde coast traffic but later migrated to other parts of the system. Although the smokebox shows what may be the effects of priming, the locomotive is clean, recalling the late David Newlands's observation that in pre-grouping times locomotives were kept at about the cleanliness of the average family car, clean but not usually spotless. (J. J. Cunningham)

Drummond '171' Class 0-4-4T No.15103 again, this time at Lybster station on the Wick and Lybster Light Railway of the Highland Section. Although it was unusual to find this particular class of locomotive off the Caledonian section, the Wick and Lybster line was limited in the weight of engine allowed and No.15103 had been moved to Inverness from Stirling in 1934 and then to Wick after the withdrawal of its predecessor on this line, ex-Highland 4-4-0T No.15013, in July 1934. The similarity of the two numbers must have caused some to look twice. This locomotive remained on the Lybster service until the line closed in 1944, after which it was withdrawn, by then the last survivor of its class. (H. C. Casserley)

usual express timing of 67 minutes. Although No.14758 was withdrawn shortly after the end of hostilities, No.14760 was not finally withdrawn until the end of 1946.

The 'Rivers' were not the only Highland locomotives to operate on Caledonian lines however, as the problem of weight restrictions on the Callander and Oban line meant that Nos.14768 *Clan McKenzie* and 17957, one of the broadly similar superheated 'Clan Goods', were tried on the line in 1933, following the withdrawal of the '55' Class 4-6-0s designed by McIntosh for that route. That was, actually, not the first time that 'Clans' had been seen south of Perth, as the fact that they fitted within the Caledonian Railway's more restrictive loading gauge meant that from June 1923 (before the Caledonian was technically part of the LMS) through working by 'Clans' between Inverness and Glasgow Buchanan Street was instituted, although that did not last long as they had difficulty maintaining time south of Perth, where they

Highland Railway 4-6-0 No.14764 Clan Munro *taking water at Dalmally station on the Callander and Oban line during its 1934-39 sojourn on the Oban route. The locomotive shed is just visible on the right. Dalmally, along with Balquhidder, was a water stop for most trains. The station was unusual on that line in that it had been rebuilt with a stone station building.* (Niall Ferguson's Collection)

occasionally needed assistance from Caledonian 4-4-0s. It was decided that the 'Clans' would be more suitable than the 'Superheated Goods' on the Oban line, and by June 1934 four examples of the class were working through to Oban, the last of the class having been transferred to Balornock shed by February 1935. Two of Peter Drummond's Highland 'Castles' (Nos.14686 *Urquhart Castle* and 14681 *Skibo Castle*) joined them, the former in August 1935 and the latter in February 1936, both having had their bogie tenders replaced with the six-wheel variety. Following a brief return to the Highland section at the beginning of 1939, the 'Castles' both went back to Oban during 1940, where they remained working mainly freight traffic until their final return to former Highland territory in 1943. The 'Clans' had already left the Oban line by then, being returned to the Highland Section in dribs and drabs between 1939 and the summer of 1940. When working over the Callander and Oban line the Highland engines had to have the height of their Manson tablet catchers altered to be compatible with those on the former Caledonian line and, of course, the alteration had to be reversed before they returned to Highland Railway metals.

Although other classes of Highland Railway engines were occasionally to be seen on Caledonian lines with excursions, before the other Caledonian locomotive classes are dealt with the only other Highland class to be transferred to former Caledonian territory will be considered. During the summer of 1935 five examples of Peter Drummond's version of the standard Drummond 0-6-0, his 'Barney', were transferred to the Glasgow area to help with the expected heavy traffic in connection with the Empire Exhibition. They were presumably chosen because they were vacuum-fitted and because they had been reboilered with Caledonian N34 boilers by the LMS, thus easing maintenance at Caledonian sheds. All five had returned north by the end of year, but in May 1939 a slightly different five were transferred to Dawsholm and Motherwell sheds, again presumably because they were vacuum-fitted, as they were exchanged for four unfitted Caledonian 0-6-0s. They, too, had returned north by the middle of 1940, but in December 1946 eight Caledonian 3F 0-6-0s from the G&SWR Section were strengthened for snowplough duties and sent north in exchange for the remaining 'Barneys', which were thought to be nearing the end of their days.

To return to Caledonian locomotives, the majority of major passenger duties were the task of the various classes of 4-4-0 which the LMS inherited in 1923. Most of them were either Drummond or McIntosh types, but one class of Brittain 4-4-0 was still in service, his 'Oban Bogie' of 1882. Ten of these had been built originally and, following reboilering by Drummond, eight had reached the LMS, but only four were repainted in LMS livery and all had gone by 1930.

The various Drummond and Lambie 4-4-0s were also fairly quick to disappear, but the McIntosh series of the various types of 'Dunalastair' 4-4-0s were powerful locomotives and still had useful years of service in them. Divided into four groups, which took their name from two named locomotives of the first and second series, No.721 *Dunalastair* and No.766 *Dunalastair 2nd*, they were to be found in both superheated and non-superheated versions. The non-superheated locomotives were the first to be scrapped and by the late 1930s the majority of them had gone, their six-wheel tenders being swapped for the bogie tenders fitted to some of the superheated types. Ladyburn, and more particularly its sub-shed Greenock (Princes Pier), became the last refuge of a number of ageing Caledonian 4-4-0s during the 1930s, where they could be employed both on passenger and freight duties on the relatively easily-graded Coast line, duties which remained well within their capabilities as they drew nearer to withdrawal.

Examples of the later series of 'Dunalastair' 4-4-0s lasted until the end of steam, and one only just missed being preserved. William Pickersgill also produced a class of superheated 4-4-0. One of them (No.124) was tested over the Midland Railway Leeds to Carlisle line in 1924 and another example was included in the Settle & Carlisle locomotive trials of 1926. Being powerful, modern locomotives they also survived into the nationalised era and were to be found all over Scotland in their latter days.

As stated above, the earlier, non-superheated, 'Dunalastairs' started to disappear from about 1930 and, with the arrival of LMS 4-4-0 Compounds in increasing numbers, even the superheated examples began to be displaced from the principal trains. The first G&SWR shed to see an allocation of Caledonian locomotives was Dumfries, which acquired the locomotives displaced when the Caledonian shed there closed in 1923, and, in addition, acquired a further significant number of 0-6-0s as early as 1928, whereas Ardrossan may have been the first to get 'Dunalastairs' when it acquired some from the nearby Caledonian shed that closed in 1931. Certainly by 1933 Ardrossan had two 'Dunalastair Is', two 'Dunalastair IIs', and one example of a 'Dunalastair III', as well as six 'Jumbos' and a single '812' Class 0-6-0. From 1932 'Dunalastairs' had begun to appear at other former G&SWR sheds such as Girvan (where 'Dunalastair III' Class No.14345 was allocated), Stranraer and Hurlford, which also had 'Jumbos'. Other Caledonian Railway 0-6-0s and '439' Class 0-4-4Ts were also making appearances at non-Caledonian sheds.

On the former Highland Railway, Caledonian locomotives took longer to make inroads. Even as late as 1937 no Caledonian locomotives at all were stationed at Aviemore or Forres but, as mentioned previously, in May 1933 Inverness had acquired 'Killin Tank' No.15001 which had previously worked the Turkey Red factory in the Vale of Leven, and the Fort George branch, near Inverness, had been worked by '439' Class No.15226 since 1935.

Apart from the reappearance of the 'River' 4-6-0s, '439' Class 0-4-4Ts were the first Caledonian locomotives to make any sustained appearance on the Highland Section, but World War II resulted in Caledonian engines arriving all over the system. Caledonian 4-4-0s, 0-6-0s and 0-6-0Ts replaced similar Highland types as the Highland locomotives aged and proved less capable of handling the increasingly heavy traffic, and by 1942 Inverness had no fewer than twelve Caledonian locomotives on its books. By 1945 there were only eight non-superheated Caledonian 4-4-0s surviving amongst the remaining 77 4-4-0s and almost all of those were to be found on Caledonian territory. The exceptions were two Pickersgill locomotives which were at Hurlford and six 'Dunalastairs' divided equally between Aviemore, Forres and Inverness, although some of the Pickersgill locomotives officially allocated to Perth were actually stationed at Blair Atholl to provide banking assistance.

Having mentioned the LMS Compound 4-4-0s, more needs to be said of their arrival on the Caledonian section. The Caledonian shed at Carlisle Kingmoor, which had quickly taken over the complement of G&SWR locomotives from that company's shed at Currock, acquired twenty Compounds in the early summer of 1925, all of which were intended to work on Scottish main lines, five being allotted to former G&SWR routes whilst the remaining fifteen were intended for the Caledonian lines. The two groups were easily distinguished as the G&SWR engines had right-hand drive whilst the others adopted Caledonian practice and were driven from the left; even so, their screw reverser must have given their drivers problems, accustomed as they were to lever reverse. With a tractive effort more than 1,000lb greater than the Pickersgill '66' Class 4-4-0s, and even more in excess of any of the superheated 4-6-0s, they proved easily equal to the tasks given them, proving able to haul the 'Midday Corridor' single-handed from Carlisle to Glasgow (except for banking over Beattock) whereas previously the train had routinely been the province of a Pickersgill 4-4-0, with another 4-4-0 assisting right through from Carlisle to Beattock Summit.

In 1927 two Compounds were allocated to Polmadie and they were soon followed by others at Carstairs, Dalry Road and Aberdeen, although responsibility for the Euston–Glasgow expresses (which, for a short period, were hauled by a pair of Compounds) soon became the duty of the new 'Royal Scots'.

The autumn of 1927 saw the first through workings of Compounds between Aberdeen and Carlisle on the 'Royal Highlander' and other trains such as the 'Postal' and

'River' Class 4-6-0 No.14759 with the smallest size of snowplough fitted on the Highland section again at Blair Atholl shed. Note that despite years in Caledonian Railway ownership it has retained the folding vacuum pipe on the front buffer beam, a characteristic Highland fitting, which has been used again after the locomotive's return to Highland territory. (Niall Ferguson's Collection)

newspaper services, Aberdeen-based 'Compounds' sharing the working with the Carlisle engines on alternate days. Additional allocations of these powerful 4-4-0s came in 1930 and 1933, but the start of the Second World War saw them in decline, with withdrawals starting in 1948.

Making the majority of its freight income from coal traffic in connection with the Lanarkshire coalfield and the associated steelworks, the Caledonian had needed a large stock of freight engines. As a result, it passed on to the LMS a considerable number of 0-6-0 tender engines and other, smaller, tank locomotives, as well as a small number of very heavy freight engines. Among the latter were the eight '600' Class 0-8-0s, which had not been a success and which were soon scrapped, the last going in 1930. There was, once again, a single class of Brittain locomotive, his '670' Class of tender goods 0-4-2, a wheel arrangement once popular in Scotland, allegedly because they could negotiate the tight curves found in docks and collieries. Of the original 30 examples, 21

reached the LMS, but only about half carried LMS livery and the last went in 1932.

The 0-6-0s were the various iterations of the standard Drummond type, copied and improved in turn by Lambie, McIntosh, and Pickersgill. Only six of the 244 'Jumbo' 0-6-0s inherited by the LMS failed to reach British Railways. Many of them had, however, been modified by the LMS. The Drummond locomotives, which could be recognised by the underhung springs on their tenders, had a modified motion fitted by the LMS, known as 'No.1 Standard Motion'. It was similar to the McIntosh motion of the later engines, which had the slidebars supported at each end and a single large balance weight at the right-hand end of the weighshaft, but 'No.1 Motion' had two small balance weights on a rearward extension of the lifting links instead. Most of the early 'Jumbos' had only steam brakes, but some of the Drummond and Lambie locomotives were fitted with Westinghouse pumps and all the McIntosh-built locomotives were Westinghouse braked. However, all the Westinghouse-fitted examples still lacked vacuum ejectors and carriage heating equipment, but that was soon remedied by the LMS.

As mentioned above, the Highland Railway 'Barney' 0-6-0s were rebuilt with the LMS standard N.34 boiler, and the same boiler was also fitted to the 'Jumbos'. It was similar to the McIntosh boiler, but with no outside clackboxes and a flatter topped dome, and was usually fitted with Ross pop valves.

A 'Beetlecrusher' dock shunting tank '492' Class 0-6-0T No.16154 inside Dawsholm shed in the early days of the grouping. The locomotive immediately behind is a 'Jubilee' 0-6-0ST which appears still to be in Caledonian Railway goods locomotive livery.
(Niall Ferguson's Collection)

The other large class of Caledonian 0-6-0 was the '300' Class built by Pickersgill. Not as attractive as the McIntosh and Drummond types, its use was confined almost entirely to freight traffic and only No.17673 was fitted with the vacuum brake. Built just after the Great War, the class was fitted with superheaters between 1927 and 1931, and the majority lasted into the early 1960s. One Caledonian oddity inherited by the LMS was the five members of the '34' Class of freight 2-6-0s. An attempt to deal with the problems associated with the cracked frames experienced by McIntosh's powerful '30' Class of passenger 0-6-0s, which resulted from their long front overhang, the provision of a leading pony truck did nothing for the appearance of one of only two classes of inside-cylindered 2-6-0s to be built in the United Kingdom, and all were withdrawn between 1935 and 1937.

Apart from tender freight engines, the Caledonian also possessed a large collection of tank engines, both passenger and goods. The commonest classes of tank engines had both been designed by McIntosh. Numerically the largest class of passenger tank was the '439' Class and its assorted variations, a number of which had been built during the early LMS period, whilst the corresponding freight tank locomotive was the '782' 0-6-0T, a numerous and powerful design, most of which lasted into the 1960s. So useful was the latter class that they prevented the ubiquitous LMS 'Jinty' tanks making any real inroads into Caledonian territory, although examples were to be found at places like Dundee and Dawsholm, which had three each. Other standard LMS designs did, of course, appear increasingly as time went by. The other powerful Caledonian shunting tank was the '498' Class with a short

wheelbase and outside cylinders, the first two examples, dating from 1911, being followed by a further 21 constructed by William Pickersgill between 1915 and 1922. Designed for shunting on dockyard and mineral lines where their short wheelbase was a major advantage, all lasted into BR days, thus demonstrating their usefulness. By the late 1920s a need for further locomotives of this type was felt, particularly on the Caledonian section, and it would have seemed logical to have built more examples of the '498' Class, particularly as the LMS had already built further examples of two other Caledonian designs, the '60' Class 4-6-0 and the Nasmyth-Wilson versions of the '439' Class 0-4-4T. However, that was not to be, and instead Horwich Works produced a locomotive superficially very similar to the '498' but with Walschaerts valve gear. The first examples appeared in 1928 and they were to be found around Merseyside and Fleetwood in Lancashire, as well as in Scotland, where they were found principally on the Clyde (there were three at Greenock, as well as six examples of the '498' Class), but they also appeared on the other side of Scotland, where two were allocated to Dalry Road shed in Edinburgh for work in Leith Docks.

The numerous 0-4-0ST 'Wee Pugs' could be found all over the Caledonian system, shunting yards and sidings (such as Dundee Docks, where they were the only locomotives allowed, and were obliged to travel at a maximum speed of 4mph, preceded by two men with red flags) and most lasted into BR days. They eventually spread far and wide, but even in the 1930s they could be found in some odd locations, such as Shrewsbury, where 16027 was working in the summer of 1936. The only other large tank locomotives were the '492'

One of the relatively small number of 'Jinty' 0-6-0Ts which reached Scotland. No.16414 is one of the three examples stationed at Dundee for shunting the extensive goods yards. It is seen here basking in the late spring sunshine on 29th May 1930. (H. C. Casserley)

'Royal Scot' Class 4-6-0 No.6143 The South Staffordshire Regiment on *the 11.00 Glasgow Central–Edinburgh Princes Street express train passing Bellshill in 1948. These and other main line locomotives were sometimes to be seen on Glasgow–Edinburgh turns in between their higher speed activity on the main line, although the non-corridor stock looks out of place behind such a locomotive.*
(J. L. Stevenson)

Class 0-8-0T and Lambie's class of 4-4-0T. Six examples of the 0-8-0T had been built in 1903-4 and were used for heavy shunting and short distance freight work. Three (Nos.16950, 16952 and 16955) were to be found at Motherwell, the last surviving until 1939, whilst another was stationed at Dundee for many years, where it assisted freight trains up the long gradient between Ninewells Junction and Fairmuir and

Maryfield goods depots, behind the Law Hill. The 4-4-0T was the only class with that wheel arrangement on the Caledonian; twelve had been built in 1893 and by LMS days had become fairly well scattered, with single examples at places such as Perth (Joint) station, where No.15024 was station pilot for many years both before and after the Grouping, and Arbroath where No.15021 could be found.

The first major class of LMS freight locomotive to appear on the Caledonian was the Hughes 2-6-0 known as a 'Crab'. The return of the 'River' Class 4-6-0s to the Highland Section (mentioned above) was facilitated by the arrival of 'Crabs' on former Caledonian lines. The first 'Crabs' to reach Scotland arrived at Perth at the end of 1928 for work on the Highland main line, but allocation to the Caledonian Section began the following year, and they were soon to be found on Perth–Glasgow passenger services. Their *métier* became the tightly timed passenger services over the Stranraer line, with its severe gradients, and they were even to be found on mineral workings in the Ayrshire coalfields. By the early

Locomotives ready for work and their cleaners posed outside Polmadie locomotive shed, with three 'Royal Scots', two 'Compounds' and a 'Jubilee' – not a Caledonian locomotive included in the line-up for the photographer. May 1935.
(T. & J. Barr Collection, Scottish Railway Preservation Society)

1930s the former Caledonian shed at Carlisle Kingmoor had ten examples and they were to be found at such diverse Caledonian locations as Aberdeen (two), Edinburgh (two), St. Rollox (four) and Polmadie (two), as well as at Carstairs, Motherwell and Stirling. Useful as they were, these outside cylinder Moguls failed to supplant the existing Caledonian 0-6-0s and 4-6-0s and it was not until the Class 5s reached the Section that the former Caledonian locomotives had serious competition on freight workings. The arrival of Class 5s in Scotland occurred in August 1934, when nine locomotives out of the first batch were sent to Perth, once again intended for use on the Highland Section, although they were also used on services between Glasgow and Perth. The problems of axle loadings on the Callander and Oban line, which had resulted in both the transfer of Highland Railway 4-6-0s and an order (subsequently cancelled) for ten smaller versions of the Class 5 with a reduced axle load, were solved by a programme of

bridge strengthening and were probably also the cause of the substitution of a 60ft turntable at Oban for the 50ft one that was previously there. Following that, the Class 5 4-6-0s became commonplace on the Oban line, and were also to be found on the Glasgow to Aberdeen expresses.

However, whilst passenger express traffic on the northern parts of the system may have been principally the preserve of Class 5s, further south express passenger trains merited more high profile motive power. The LMS introduced the 'Royal Scot' class of three-cylinder 4-6-0 to the public in 1927. Contracts for construction were given to the North British Locomotive Company in Glasgow, who divided work between two of their Glasgow sites at Queens Park and Hyde Park Works. The new locomotives (which had been allocated to power classification 6P) were displayed to the public amid great publicity at various exhibitions around Scotland, such as that at Glasgow Central station in October 1927 when No.6127 (later *Novelty*) was placed at Platform 1. The locomotive was internally lit and 14,000 people paid to see the new engine over three days – the money taken going to charity. Similar events were held at Edinburgh Princes Street (where 10,000 people turned up) and at Dundee. Locomotives Nos.6127-6132 were allocated to Polmadie shed and *Novelty* was regularly driven by David Gibson until his retirement in 1929.

LMS-built 4-4-0 No. 1141 at Polmadie on 27th October 1945. By this time Compounds had generally been withdrawn from use on the highest profile trains, but were still useful engines for a wide range of other duties.
(H. C. Casserley)

In 1928 'The Royal Scot' stopped at Symington, so a non-stop London–Glasgow service to rival the 392.9 miles of the LNER London–Edinburgh 'Flying Scotsman' was not possible. There appear to have been two reasons for the stop at Symington. The principal reason was to divide the train into its Edinburgh and Glasgow portions but also it was a chance to take on water, there being no troughs on the Caledonian Section at that date. However, a few days before the heavily publicised 'Flying Scotsman' was to start on 1st May 1928, the LMS ran 'The Royal Scot' in two parts. The Glasgow portion was hauled by 'Royal Scot' locomotive No.6113 for the 401.4 miles, whilst the Edinburgh train was hauled by LMS Compound No.1054 for its 399.7-mile journey, both trains thus breaking the LNER record in advance. Although the length of the Glasgow run has since been beaten, the Edinburgh run remains a record for a 4-4-0 locomotive! Non-stop running from Euston to Glasgow had to wait for the installation of water troughs on the Caledonian main line. That occurred in 1927-8 with three sets of troughs being installed at New Cumnock, Floriston and near Strawfrank Junction in the vicinity of Carstairs.

Before William Stanier arrived from Swindon in 1932 the LMS had already authorised what was officially termed (probably for accounting purposes) a reconstruction of the LNWR 'Claughton' 4-6-0s, but which was really the construction of a new class of locomotive, the examples of which rapidly became known as 'Baby Scots' or, officially, 'Patriots'. Stanier soon authorised the construction of a further fifteen, but then decided to fit the last ten with tapered boilers. Thus the first of what became the 'Jubilee' Class 4-6-0 appeared in April 1934, with no fewer than 113 examples in service by April 1935.

Although the 'Jubilees' did most of their work south of the border, there was a small number allocated to Scottish sheds. The first examples arrived at Polmadie in January 1935 with a couple reaching Perth in November of the same year. Between 1935 and 1948 'Jubilees' were never in Scotland in any great numbers or, indeed, permanently at any former Caledonian location except Carlisle Kingmoor, which had eleven in 1937, sixteen in 1941 and seventeen in 1948.

By the summer of 1930 Polmadie had six passenger diagrams for Class 6 locomotives, three to Carlisle and three to Crewe, returning the next day. New rolling stock was introduced to complement the new locomotives and passengers enjoyed plush upholstered seats, real wood veneer walls and unobstructed views from the windows.

It seemed that nothing would better the performances of the 'Royal Scot' locomotives over the London to Glasgow route, but in 1937 the LMS introduced the 'Coronation' Class of Pacific locomotive which was also exhibited to the public at various locations, including Glasgow Central station. On 26th February 1939 one of the class, No.6234 *Duchess of Abercorn,* recently fitted with a double-exhaust system, repeated a test run it had made two weeks previously, on Sunday 12th, from Crewe to Glasgow and back There was a poor start from Crewe, with time lost from speed restrictions, but north of Carlisle things became much better with the 39.7miles to Beattock station managed in only 39 minutes 40seconds, an average speed of 60mph from start to passing Beattock. A further 16½ minutes were taken for the climb to the summit, followed by an easy descent to Symington, where a stop for water was taken even though Strawfrank troughs were only six miles further on and should have been easily reachable. After a two hour turnaround at

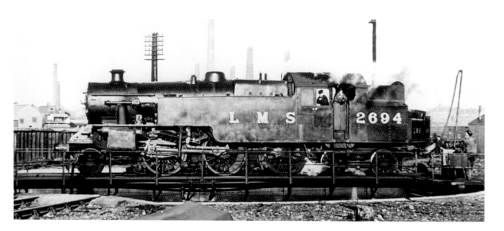

Despite the Locomotive Department's initial rejection of the vacuum-driven turntable at Polmadie in the early 1930s, one was fairly soon installed there. Fairburn 2-6-4T No.2694 is shown here being turned at Polmadie, using the vacuum tractor. (J. L. Stevenson)

Glasgow, which almost certainly involved a trip to Polmadie to refill the tender, the return trip started with another good climb to Motherwell, followed by a high-speed dash between Symington and Beattock Summit, which was passed at 62mph despite the 1 in 99 climb.

However, the advent of the Second World War meant that construction of further examples of the class was considerably delayed. After the original five, a further ten were built in 1938, but of the twenty authorised in 1938 for construction in 1939, only five appeared, with a further five of the same batch being built in 1940. No further examples appeared until 1943, when four more entered service, the same number also appearing in 1944. By that time, the locomotive situation on the LMS was better than it had been at any time since 1939 as far as numbers available was concerned, but the state of the locomotives and the poor quality of fuel available (mainly because of the demands of the Royal Navy) meant that the service provided and the mechanical condition and outward appearance of the locomotive stock was extremely poor. Throughout the LMS system locomotives that were destined for withdrawal (and which in some cases had actually been withdrawn) were overhauled and kept in service, and that was particularly true on the Caledonian section, where classes such as the 'River' and '191' 4-6-0s were kept in service despite being well past their 'sell by' date.

However, once the war was over, efforts were soon underway to restore normality, although the problems resulting from that conflict may have been the reason for some unusual visitors to the area. In 1946 four ex-LNWR 2-4-2Ts came north, possibly because they were motor-fitted. Two of them were stationed at the former G&SWR shed at Dumfries, from where they worked the Lockerbie branch, whilst the other two were stabled at Hamilton, one being withdrawn from there the same year, whilst the other moved to Beattock, where it was used on the Moffat branch. All had been withdrawn by 1950.

During 1945 an additional nineteen 2-6-2Ts had arrived at former Caledonian mpds to supplement the ten already working on the Glasgow low level lines. Of those new allocations, six went to Hamilton, and no fewer than eleven to Dawsholm, where there were also three examples of Pickersgill's 4-6-2T. The Pickersgill engines soon left to work as banking engines at Beattock, where they were joined by the single 4-6-2T of the same class from Greenock (Ladyburn), it being replaced by another example of the new Fairburn 2-6-4T. 'Black Fives' were by now common, with Motherwell having twenty on its books in 1947, as well as eighteen '60' Class 4-6-0s. The need to work heavy freight from the industrial belt of Central Scotland had meant that Motherwell had also acquired a number of 8F 2-8-0s during the latter years of the war, and although some were quick to go (including the Westinghouse-fitted War Department examples) seven were still there in 1947.

Despite the twenty at Motherwell, the stronghold of 'Black Fives' in Scotland was probably Perth, which by 1947 had no fewer than 60 examples allocated. The class had been found increasingly versatile and had even replaced the 8F 2-8-0s that had been allocated to Perth during the war.

The years after the war would also see Caledonian locomotives move south of the border. Late in 1946 Caledonian 0-4-4Ts Nos.15130 and 15192 were allocated to Ilkley/Manningham in Yorkshire to work over the Wharfedale line, replacing 0-4-4Ts Nos.1902 and 1903 which were transferred to Bath. In May 1947 those the two Caledonian engines were replaced at Manningham by two others (Nos.15169 and 15227) which stayed until August 1948, at which time they were moved to Dundee. That was, actually, not the first time that the class had worked in England, as Nos.15264 and 15266 had been allocated to the Nottingham area in 1932/3.

This dispersal of Caledonian locomotives throughout the Scottish LMS system – and even across the border – would, of course, seem nothing compared with the reallocation of engines in Scotland that would follow nationalisation in 1948.

Carriage Stock

Although the Caledonian Railway had already operated Pullman vehicles off its own network when, in June 1922, one of the cars delivered that year, *Lady Nairn*, had been rostered on the 10.10am from Glasgow Buchanan Street to Aviemore, on the Highland Railway, returning from there to Glasgow on the 3.30pm ex-Inverness, the formation of the LMS extended the area of operation for the Pullman vehicles to include the entire LMS Scottish area, encompassing the lines of the Highland and G&SWR as well as that of the Caledonian. In addition to *Lady Nairn* continuing to run north of Perth, two of the 1923 cars were put into service over the former G&SWR route to Ayr, whilst Car No.80, a third class buffet car built by Clayton Wagons Ltd. of Lincoln, joined the Pullman observation car *Maid of Morven* as an additional vehicle on the Oban route during June, July and August, working from Glasgow to Oban on the 5.10pm train, arriving at 9.10pm. In the other direction it left Oban for Glasgow at 11.15am, *Maid of Morven* working from Glasgow at 9.15am, and from Oban at 3.35pm. Car No.80 last appears in the LMS Scottish Timetable in the summer of 1927, still rostered to run between Glasgow Buchanan Street and Oban, but by 1928 No.80 had been renumbered into the Southern Railway Pullman series as Third Class Car No.27, presumably as a result of the arrival in Scotland of no fewer than six new Pullmans. Those resulted from a new agreement being signed between the Pullman Car Co. and the LMS in 1927. Of the six, three (*Queen Margaret*, *Kate Dalrymple* and *Helen of Mar*) were completely new vehicles, constructed by the Metropolitan company, but the others were cars which had previously run on the Great Eastern Railway as 21-seat buffet cars (named respectively *Nevada*, *Columbia* and *Atlanta*) and been converted into 27 seat dining cars arranged in a 2:1 pattern to conform to the standard LMS seating layout at that time.

The Pullman Company was not, however, content merely to get further vehicles on to the LMS rails in Scotland and, with its Caledonian Railway contract (which had been taken over by the LMS) due to expire in 1933, it attempted to get the LMS to agree to an entirely new all-Pullman service between Euston and Edinburgh and Glasgow to rival the LNER 'Queen of Scots' Pullman.

Not only were they unsuccessful with that and a number of related but less expensive proposals but, when the existing contract expired in 1933, the LMS refused to renew it, and the Pullman Company found itself with little option but to sell the 22 Scottish Pullmans to the LMS at a knockdown price. Therefore, on Monday 4th December 1933 the LMS took over the ownership of all the Pullman Company's vehicles which were running on their routes in Scotland, the catering staff, who were retained by the LMS, and the catering facilities, which became the responsibility of the hotel division of the company. The vehicles remained in Pullman livery until due for a routine repaint, although all were allocated numbers in the LMS carriage sequence and some certainly carried that number in addition to their name. All the pre-war vehicles had been built on wooden underframes rather than the steel underframes of the later ones, and were in such a poor state that all had been disposed of by the end of 1937. The remaining vehicles were once again withdrawn from service at the outbreak of the Second World War (although there are rumours that they were used to transport various VIPS on 'war service'). All were returned to service in 1945 and lasted into nationalisation, being withdrawn at various dates until the last six were scrapped in 1961.

Although this volume concerns principally only the former Caledonian Railway it must be remembered that the LMS operated the three former Scottish lines it had absorbed as a single entity, and in 1931 it was decided that the Locomotive and Carriage & Wagon Departments should be amalgamated and their work rationalised. As a result the carriage repair work that had been carried out at the former Highland Railway Locomotive Works at Lochgorm, Inverness, was moved to the Caledonian Works at St. Rollox in Glasgow and Needlefield Carriage and Wagon Shops at Inverness were in future only used for carriage cleaning purposes.

The Caledonian was, of course, a Westinghouse-braked company and, although a number of vehicles (mainly non-passenger coaching stock, together with composites and brake-composites used on through services) were dual-braked to permit use on other companies' lines (both the Highland Railway and the Glasgow & South Western had used the vacuum brake) the decision of the LMS to adopt the vacuum brake, which had been used by the majority of its constituents, meant that most of the former Caledonian carriages were restricted to services on that company's lines unless they were converted.

By 1927 the Clyde Coast services out of Glasgow were the province of vacuum braked stock, mainly 57 foot bogie vehicles, except for one set of six-wheelers. At the same date, the LMS trains on the Dundee and Arbroath Joint Line continued to be Westinghouse braked although the LNER stock used on that line was vacuum fitted.

The year 1933 saw the commencement of a major conversion programme for the fitting of vacuum brakes to all suitable LMS carriages. That meant that those carriages deemed unsuitable for conversion were consigned to very much secondary services or branch line use. In effect that meant that only electrically-lit carriages were converted, gas-lit ones being consigned to secondary use. In fact by the end of 1932 all Caledonian-built six-wheel carriages except two or three had been withdrawn and, although some vacuum-fitted six-wheelers are shown in the summer 1933 *Passenger Train Marshalling Arrangements* as being used on workmen's trains, these were, presumably, carriages from another of the LMS constituent companies that had been transferred to the Caledonian Section as they were in a better state of repair, a common procedure. A small number of 45ft carriages remained in use after 1933, some even receiving their second LMS numbers (a renumbering of all LMS carriage stock being part of the process), but all except one had gone by the end of 1938, only brake third No.24186 (originally Caledonian 1163 of 1897) bizarrely lasting until March 1945. With their later examples electrically-lit the 48ft coaches fared slightly better, but none was converted to vacuum brakes and the majority had gone by the start of the Second World War, although a small number, having survived that conflict, continued in service for a few years longer.

Most of the 50ft and all the 57ft carriages were of much more recent construction of course, and the 57ft vehicles in particular complemented the standard length of LMS carriages: all were converted to vacuum brake, and almost all lasted into the days of British Railways. The same was also true of the 65ft and 68ft 'Grampian' stock, the Westinghouse-braked vehicles being converted, whilst those vehicles already dual-fitted would have had their Westinghouse fixtures removed as opportunity permitted.

As for the conversions themselves, there appear to have been two different arrangements used with no obvious reason why one method was chosen for a particular vehicle rather than the other. One arrangement used two conventional LMS-style vacuum cylinders and often, but not always, also involved replacement of the battery boxes, whilst the other method retained the original battery boxes with the addition of a large horizontal vacuum cylinder.

The LMS, with a small number of exceptions, one of which is noted below, adopted 57ft as the standard length for its passenger carriages. In addition, the LMS tended to use newly constructed vehicles to replace individual carriages within sets, rather than replacing the whole set. The first of such vehicles to be replaced were usually composites (the LMS built very few first class carriages), thus giving the benefit of up-to-date vehicles to the wealthier passengers with more expensive tickets. Therefore, although it is relatively easy to spot such carriages in photographs (especially the Period II and III stock with flush sides), unless 57ft carriages are shown in the marshalling circulars to be Westinghouse fitted, it is often difficult to know whether particular carriages are of Caledonian or LMS origin.

The *Passenger Train Marshalling Arrangements* from 1st June 1933 show that 57ft vacuum fitted carriages (either LMS built or Caledonian ones) made up by far the majority of train formation off main line routes, the commonest formation being either two brake thirds plus a composite, or two brake thirds plus a first class carriage and an all-third. The one unusual exception to that was on the Cathcart Circle line in Glasgow, where the tight clearances meant that 57ft carriages had proved unsuitable as replacements for the Caledonian four-wheel stock that traditionally worked the route. As a result eight sets of LMS-built 54ft vehicles (plus spares) were allocated to the services. Seven sets were supplied by Hurst Nelson, and one set plus eight spare vehicles by Pickering & Co. in 1926. Each set consisted of five vehicles (brake third/composite/first/composite/brake third), the composites being only 51ft long, and provided 160 first class and 264 third class seats. Although these carriages were introduced during what is commonly known as the LMS Period I, characterised by fully-panelled wooden-bodied vehicles, the

A first class example of William Pickersgill's 30ft four-wheel coaches built for the Balerno branch but actually used more widely in the Edinburgh area. No.26056 was built in 1921 and is seen at Barnton station on 2nd October 1946. This carriage, along with all the others of the same length, was withdrawn from service on 10th May 1952.
(H. C. Casserley)

The interior of a post-war LMS third class sleeper. Having introduced third class sleepers somewhat belatedly in 1928, the railways made no attempt to provide similar facilities to the first class version — third class passengers got a pillow and blanket and were able to lie down but were expected to sleep fully clothed. These lasted until the 1960s when BR Mark I sleepers arrived, the arrangements providing sheets and permitting what were then second class passengers to sleep normally. (LMS official)

Cathcart Circle coaches were built with steel panelling, and may be considered as the prototypes for the Period II vehicles, particularly as the firsts and composites had five-a-side seating. Unlike the Period II vehicles, however, they were initially painted in a false fully-panelled style, with painted waist panels. In the years before the Second World War nine of the composite carriages were downgraded to thirds, the first class being dealt with in a similar manner during the war years, whilst the remaining composites were not downgraded until 1953.

Further away from the central belt services were often still provided by Westinghouse-fitted (rather than vacuum) stock, some of the remaining 45ft and 48ft stock being found on services out of Dundee West where some other very strange sets were to be found, such as Set No.331, which worked between Perth and Arbroath via Forfar, and Set No.335, working between Dundee West and Blairgowrie (with an occasional trip to Stanley Junction) which each consisted of a 57ft brake third carriage coupled to a 65ft brake composite. Dundee seems to have been a stronghold of the Caledonian 65ft carriages, as they were also to be found working over the jointly owned Dundee & Arbroath Line, where the two LMS Sets consisted entirely of carriages of that length (brake third/composite/first/third/brake third respectively).

The LMS was keen on open (which the company referred to as vestibuled) carriages rather than side-corridor vehicles for its principal trains, especially on Anglo-Scottish services. Therefore 'The Royal Scot' and 'The Midday Scot' (the 10.00am and 1.30pm daily departures from Euston) were almost entirely composed of modern stock and from 1928 included a lounge brake which was exclusively for the use of first class passengers, together with a semi-open first. The discussions concerning the extension of the Pullman contract, and the possible use of Pullmans on cross-border services were resolved by the introduction in July 1937 of 'The Coronation Scot'. It, too, ran between Euston and Glasgow Central, with departures leaving at 1.30pm in each direction. The trains were composed entirely of Stanier Period III flush sided stock, with a corridor brake first and third at each end,

between which were two full kitchen cars flanked by 42-seat vestibule coaches of respective class, together with one corridor first with two-a-side seating. Even so, these carriages were simply examples of standard LMS stock which had refitted interiors and which had been equipped with pressure ventilation.

Prior to 1928 sleeping car accommodation had been entirely the preserve of first class passengers, but in that year both the LMS and the LNER introduced it for third class passengers, necessitating the construction of appropriate vehicles. Unlike 'The Royal', 'Midday' and 'Coronation Scots', sleeping car services also ran between Euston and Perth, Dundee West, Aberdeen and Oban, as well as between Birmingham, Liverpool, Manchester and Glasgow Central and, within Scotland, between Glasgow Buchanan Street and Inverness.

Apart from the cross-border services, and when operated in conjunction with a dining car, it would appear that few open carriages were to be found on Caledonian metals, one exception being the 9.45am train from Glasgow to Oban and its 3.40pm return working which, following withdrawal of the Pullman observation car *Maid of Morven* in December 1937, was composed of vestibule vehicles.

A rare interior view of the Pullman observation car Maid of Morven *in service, entering Loch Awe station. The movable armchairs and curtained panoramic windows are well displayed. The seated lady is Mrs. Casserley on her honeymoon!* (H. C. Casserley)

Details of Scottish Pullman Cars acquired by the Caledonian Railway and the LMS

Name	Entered Service	Type	LMS No.	Repainted by LMS	Withdrawn
Mary Hamilton	1914	Buffet Car	200	October 1934	November 1937
Mary Beaton	1914	Buffet Car	201	January 1936	October 1936
Mary Seaton	1914	Buffet Car	202		February 1936
Mary Carmichael	1914	Buffet Car	203	March 1936	October 1936
Annie Lawrie	1914	Buffet Car	204	February 1934	November 1937
Helen MacGregor	1914	Buffet Car	205	May 1935	February 1936
Flora MacDonald	1914	Dining Car	206	November 1934	October 1937
Fair Maid of Perth	1914	Dining Car	207	1935	December 1937
Lass o' Gowrie	1914	Dining Car	208	November 1934	October 1937
Maid of Morven	1914	Buffet Observation	209	October 1936	December 1937
Duchess of Gordon	1919	Dining Car	210		December 1937
Jeanie Deans	1927	Dining Car	211	March 1935	August 1948
Jenny Geddes	1927	Dining Car	212	August 1934	May 1955
Diana Vernon	1927	Dining Car	213	December 1934	March 1955
Lady Nairn	1922	Dining Car	214	May 1936	December 1960
Bonnie Jean	1922	Dining Car	215	February 1936	May 1955
Lass o' Ballochmyle	1923	First Dining	216	December 1934	January 1961
Meg Dods	1923	First Dining	217	November 1935	May 1961
Mauchline Belle	1923	First Dining	218	November 1934	April 1961
Queen Margaret	1927	Dining Car	219	July 1936	May 1961
Kate Dalrymple	1927	Dining Car	220	November 1935	April 1961
Helen of Mar	1927	Dining Car	221	June 1934	July 1958
Car No.80	1923	Third Buffet Car			Moved 1927

New uses for old carriage trucks. A trailer for a mechanical horse on a six-wheeler open carriage truck. (Niall Ferguson's Collection)

Non-passenger Rolling Stock

Another exception to the wholesale clearance of elderly carriages was, of course, the non-passenger coaching stock (NPCS) vehicles, such as passenger brake vans, horseboxes and milk and fruit vans. Such vehicles had usually been dual-braked when built and consequently continued to be available for traffic without alteration. As a result they sometimes had very long lives, many lasting well into the BR period.

Private owner wagons were still a major item on the railways in the LMS era, as was the transport of coal, although the traffic was well below pre-war levels. By the time the LMS took over, the worst of the private owner wagons had been eliminated. The Caledonian had tried in to buy out the private owners in the nineteenth century but found this to be beyond it. Shotts colliery wagons are seen here bringing coal to the S.S. Nieuwland *at Grangemouth. The* Nieuwland *was to be sunk by German E-boats in the North Sea on 4th September 1940.* (Niall Ferguson's Collection)

The same was also true of goods vehicles, although their history, even during the Caledonian period, is poorly recorded. The origins of the Caledonian Railway had been in the mineral railways of mid-Lanark and throughout the life of the company it was predominantly a mineral and goods railway. In the final year of independent operation 58% of its revenue was derived from transporting those commodities. The wagon stock, naturally, reflected the predominance of that traffic with 28,251 or 55% of the wagon stock classed as mineral wagons in addition to which no fewer than 1,279 of the service vehicles were allocated for the conveyance of loco-motive coal.

The Directors' Report for 31st December 1922 gave the total wagon stock as 51,536 with 1,778 service vehicles in addition. The wagon fleet had peaked at 65,731 vehicles in 1907 but the replacement of small-capacity wagons with wagons rated for 30, 40 and even 50 tons saw a steady reduction in the fleet size, whilst increasing the overall carrying capacity. At the grouping the wagons of less than 8 tons capacity comprised only 269 open goods wagons, 1,779 covered goods and 367 mineral wagons, less than 5% of the total.

A range of wagons had also been developed for the iron and steel industries ranging from those for pig iron to rail wagons, and there were also special bogie wagons for conveying exceptionally heavy loads. Other general goods traffic was handled in conventional open wagons and covered vans. Cattle wagons were part of the goods stock but the meat, fish, fruit, milk and refrigerator vans were mainly classed as non passenger coaching stock.

There is no known surviving register of wagons for either the LMS or pre-grouping periods so we have no record of the actual stock make up by wagon number or of how the

A Caledonian 20-ton six-wheel goods brake in LMS days. These useful vans had cast iron slabs in them to give them the right weight . This one is showing the beginnings of a tendency the type had of the frames' becoming curved downwards towards the ends. Note that the LMS was denied the opportunity of symmetrically placing the letters of the company's initials. (Niall Ferguson's Collection)

CR and LMS vehicle numbers were related. It has been generally accepted that the LMS added 300,000 to the Caledonian number up to 352,999 which should have been more than adequate for the number of wagons transferred. However, the Caledonian had numbered the goods and mineral stock beyond 74,000 and at the time of the Grouping there must have been at least 20,000 blank or unused numbers in the Caledonian Register.

The Caledonian had numbered various parts of its wagon stock from '1' up, such as its gunpowder vans, the special heavy weight wagons and the goods wagons. To eliminate this duplication and to accommodate those wagons carrying CR numbers greater than 53,000 these must all have been renumbered into blank CR numbers before adding the 300,000. This renumbering therefore applied to almost half the wagon stock, and the actual details of how it was done have disappeared from the historical record. It is therefore unreliable to derive CR numbers by deducting 300,000 from an LMS wagon number. The only documented examples of how the wagons were renumbered are:

i) The LMS diagrams for the special wagons which confirm that each CR number had 300,000 added.

ii) A series of tables based on bogie type, including the 30 ton bogie mineral wagons, which records that these wagons were randomly renumbered before the 300,000 was added. Brake vans and service vehicles were numbered from 353,000 upwards.

Obviously the grouping saw the introduction of standard designs of LMS wagons to replace the pre-existing Caledonian ones as those became increasingly dilapidated, but this was a piecemeal process. What did change, however, was the traffic carried. During the 1920s as a result of falling international markets, particularly in Eastern Europe, but also because of the exhaustion of the high quality seams in the Lanarkshire coalfield, there was a considerable reduction in coal production in Scotland. That meant, therefore, that the withdrawal of Caledonian-built mineral wagons did not produce a need for replacement wagons, the traffic reducing in parallel with the reduction in wagons. The result was that large numbers of Caledonian wagons could still be still be seen well into the BR era, as could other examples of Caledonian-built wagons and vans, although in their case the move to faster, fitted freight trains meant that Caledonian vehicles (which were in general unfitted) became obsolescent whilst still not life-expired and tended to be transferred to Departmental use.

6

Out and About with the LMS

Economic Realities

On 26th May 1924 the Railway Rates Tribunal opened to consider the 'standard' revenue of the four amalgamated companies. This stemmed from the Railways Act 1921 and was intended to form a defence against any monopolistic influences resulting from the Grouping. In the event the economic and competitive circumstances meant that the grouped companies did not attain this 'standard' revenue, for on the whole their dividend payments were low or non-existent. The accompanying tables show the income and expenditure data for the LMS railway undertaking, with the effects of the general strike in 1926 obvious. Apart from 1926, however, the economy was reasonably sound until the depression of the early 1930s. Fortunately this was followed by a recovery until the war changed things.

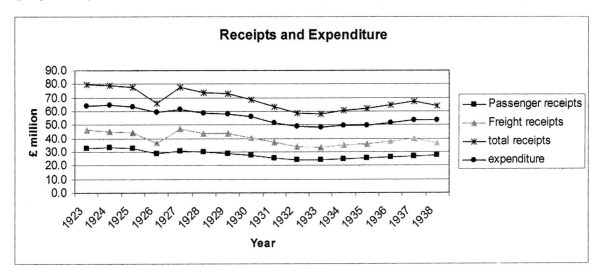

This shows the basic difficulties with which the LMS had to cope. They are even more obvious when we look at the dividends paid, especially when we note that in 1932–1934 and 1938 full interest was not even paid on the preference shares.

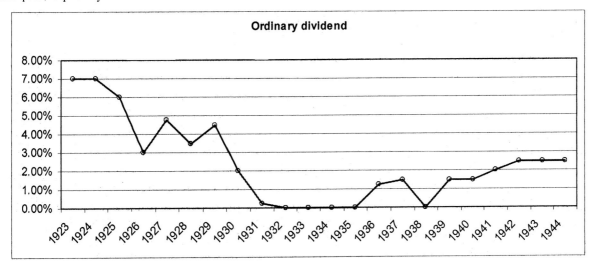

The LMS annual report noted a falling-off in revenue in 1926, particularly in minerals and heavy goods. Towards the end of 1928 railways and the unions agreed a 2½% reduction in pay on the railways, affecting all staff from the General Managers downwards. The directors subsequently applied the same cut to their payments. That year the LMS shareholders' meeting noted a loss of income due to the industrial depression, road competition and fare reductions made to meet the road competition. The main effect was a reduction in freight caused by the depression, but it is conspicuous that, although the passenger revenue held up, there was a significant shift away from ordinary fares toward excursion and weekend fares, another effect of the competition.

The LMS had other business interests: its catering (hotels, refreshment rooms and restaurant cars), shipping interests, docks and harbours, investments in road transport, canals, and latterly air transport. The shipping interests, mainly in Scotland and the Irish Sea, generally showed a surplus of £200,000 or more annually in the 1930s and the hotels and catering were rather more profitable. Road transport was a loss-maker until 1930, after which it turned in surpluses, but the canals and air transport always showed losses, as did the docks in all but four years. Overall the ancillary activities contributed a little to the company's profits except for a few years around 1930.

These statistics about the LMS show the hard economic pressures, despite which the railway improved the services and rolling stock on most of its surviving passenger services. The company's ordinary stock value had shrunk from £101.25 to £35 between 1923 and 1937. In that year 1937 the railway carried 4 million first class, 235 million third class passengers and 91 million workmen, along with 215,141 annual season ticket holders, and a few thousand second class passengers. (The few remaining second class services were not in Scotland.) The tracks were shared by 30 million tons of goods and 109 million of minerals.

After the formation of the LMS there was some mixing of the stock of the constituent companies. A Caledonian 0-6-0, still sporting CR livery, heads a freight eastwards out of Annan (G&SWR) station. The composition of the freight, with a predominance of sheeted open wagons, is typical of the pre-grouping period, but was to change in LMS times. Notice the distinctive home signal for Annan station, with the lower arm having its spectacle to the left of the post, presumably to simplify the lamping arrangements. Although this was a G&SWR example, fairly soon changed to a standard CR-pattern arm by the LMS, the CR had had some similar examples. (J. J. Cunningham)

Steamer Services

With the formation of the LMS the Caledonian and the G&SWR shipping fleets presented that new company with a dilemma. The Caledonian Steam Packet Co. (CSPC), had been a wholly-owned subsidiary of the CR, whereas the G&SWR steamers had been part of the railway company and thus passed directly into LMS ownership. Those different relationships were maintained under the LMS but, even so, the steamers owned by the two companies were treated as one fleet with a corporate identity, characterised by a new funnel colour, which did not make its first appearance until July 1923, the official date of the CR joining the LMS. The new colour was an attempt to merge the colours of the two constituent fleets and consisted of a yellow funnel with a thick black top, divided from the yellow by a red band. Unfortunately the result was considered by most as far from attractive and was misconstrued as further evidence of Midland Railway influence over the new company. In 1924 new hull colours also appeared almost identical to the Caledonian one of black with a white boot topping and red lower hull, but with white deck saloons in the style of the

G&SWR, rather than the pale pink and light blue favoured by the CR. For the 1925 season the 'tartan chimneys' were also abandoned and a return made to the plain yellow of the Caledonian era, a livery that would remain unchanged from then onwards. In the same year Charles Bremner, Manager and Secretary of the CSPC, became LMS Marine Superintendent (Northern Division) and all the office staff were transferred to Gourock, as that pier was wholly owned by the LMS. Within a relatively short period of time it became apparent that the former G&SWR steamers were in a much poorer state of repair than their CR counterparts, probably as a result of skimping on maintenance during the years prior to the amalgamation. By 1923 the *Glen Sannox* had to be replaced as the cost of reboilering was prohibitive and a new turbine steamer of the same name, a copy of the Caledonian *Duchess of Argyll,* joined the LMS fleet for the June 1925 season. By the spring of 1925 the *Glen Rosa* was also nearing the end of her days, and by the following year only the former G&SWR *Atalanta* still had a valid boiler certificate.

Late in 1928 Parliament recommended that the LMS and Coast Lines Ltd. jointly acquire David MacBrayne Ltd, both owning 50%. This became David MacBrayne (1928) Ltd. late in 1928, with a main board in London, although the real business was done by the Glasgow board. The Glasgow board had a representative of MacBrayne's Ltd., three members from Coast Lines Ltd. and three, Messrs. Argile, Bremner and Killin, from the LMS. Robert Killin, then the General Superintendent for the LMS Northern Division, was Chairman. The new company quickly put in an order for five new steamers and began to discuss the vexed question of Sunday excursion traffic. The LMS was able to coordinate some business with MacBrayne's but, on the whole, the two operations were distinct, although with some common problems such as the threat of road competition.

This gave the LMS a small share of the lucrative excursion trade, in addition to the 2½ million passengers it carried each year on the Clyde Coast, and in the summer of 1930 a one-class turbine steamer named *Duchess of Montrose* started to provide cruises from Gourock. The limitation of routes available to the former G&SWR company resulting from its original Act of Parliament meant that new vessels were added to the CSPC fleet, and over the following years the G&SWR fleet dwindled as a result, the turbine-powered *Duchess of Hamilton* (replacing the G&SWR *Juno*) joining the CSPC in 1932. Replacement of the old paddle steamers increased in pace from that date with *Mercury* (another G&SWR boat) and *Caledonia* being replaced with new paddle vessels in 1934, both the new vessels joining the CSPC fleet.

The LMS took full advantage of the drop in price for new vessels resulting from the Depression and in 1936 two new paddle steamers, *Atalanta* and *Jupiter,* replaced the last remaining G&SWR paddle boats, also joining the CSPC fleet. With more people holidaying in the UK, traffic continued to rise and in 1935 no fewer than 3 million passengers were carried. In that year, too, the last completely independent steamer operator on the Clyde, the 'White Funnel Fleet', of John Williamson Ltd. and Turbine Steamers Ltd., which had some of the fastest vessels on the Clyde, was taken over by the LMS, CSPC and MacBrayne. The turbine steamers were *Queen Mary* (1933), *King George V* (1926), *Queen Alexandra* (1912) and *King Edward* (1901) – the first turbine on the Clyde. *King George V* and *Queen Alexandra* went to MacBrayne and were put on the Bridge Wharf–Tarbert–Ardrishaig–Inveraray run, and the route to Campbeltown; the rest went to the LMS/CSPC. At the same time the LMS took over the Gourock–Kilcreggan ferry. In 1938 the *Glen Rosa,* the last surviving G&SWR steamer, was transferred to the CSPC and, as both the CSPC and MacBrayne's were officially independent companies, the LMS lost its direct link with maritime traffic on the Clyde Coast.

The year 1938 was the pre-war swansong of the Clyde Coast steamers. The summer of the following year saw the outbreak of war and within weeks thirteen ships, all paddle steamers, were called up for war service, six from the CSPC, three from its subsidiary, Williamson-Buchanan, and four from the LNER. Two turbine steamers and four smaller CSPC vessels also saw wartime service, but stayed on the Clyde, being put into service as tenders for the vast number of troopships using the river. Three of the older vessels, helped by their shallower draft, took part in the Dunkirk evacuation. Whilst minesweeping was a common duty, the more modern vessels often ended up as anti-aircraft vessels. Unlike during the previous conflict, civilian holidays continued to be allowed, although the numbers who actually went 'doon the watter' dropped substantially. However, because of the reduced number of steamers available, now all repainted in austere wartime grey, long queues formed and boats and their connecting trains were full to overflowing. Rationing meant that foodstuffs were in short supply and those who neglected to bring their own sandwiches soon found that the bakers and cafeterias had sold out.

The end of the war saw the surviving vessels (three LMS steamers had been lost in action) once again in a poor state of repair, but the numbers of passengers carried continued at the wartime level of approximately two million per annum. Then, on 1st January 1948, the British Transport Commission took over control of the former LNER steamers whilst the CSPC took over responsibility for their day-to-day operation whilst continuing to operate both its own fleet and the former Williamson-Buchanan ships, which were now fully integrated with it. In November 1951, the former LNER boats were also transferred to the CSPC. Thus the Caledonian Railway's wholly owned subsidiary company had taken over all the railway operated steamers on the Clyde and continued to operate, albeit as a shadow of its former glory, until it in its turn was merged with the company operating services to the Western Isles, forming Caledonian MacBrayne in 1973.

The Clyde Coast was not, however, the only stretch of water on which the LMS operated steamers in Scotland. Some of the larger inland Lochs also had steamer services, and the

LMS became involved with these as well. On Loch Tay steamer services had commenced in 1882 with the Marquis of Breadalbane's founding of a company which built two vessels, *Lady of the Lake* and *Sybilla*, at Kenmore. Two further vessels followed within a few years, followed by *Queen of the Lake* in 1907. The last three all passed to the CSPC in 1922 but *Lady of the Lake* and *Sybilla* were broken up at Kenmore in 1929, leaving just *Queen of the Lake* to provide the service through the 1930s until the outbreak of war, the service not resuming in 1945. The service ran from Loch Tay pier (by the station of the same name) to Kenmore, there being bus connections from Kenmore to the railway at Aberfeldy.

Loch Awe is the third largest fresh water loch in Scotland and had a number of steamers. The first were those of Messrs. Hutcheson, later MacBrayne, but their last vessel, the *Lochawe*, was laid up during the First World War, and was scrapped in 1925 without resuming service. Other ships were owned by Duncan Fraser of the Lochawe Hotel, with *Countess of Breadalbane*, a single screw steamer, with saloons fore and aft, somewhat similar in general design to *Lady of the Lake* built in the same year for service on Loch Tay. This service was also taken over by the CSPC in 1922, with two ships, *Countess of Breadalbane* and *Growley*. These ran services between Loch Awe station and Ford or Taycreggan respectively at the start of the LMS period, only the one to Ford remaining at the start of the war in 1939. The first *Countess of Breadalbane* was broken up in 1936, but was replaced by a motor vessel of the same name, also owned by CSPC.

In connection with the steamer service on Loch Awe the LMS started two bus services in the Oban area in July 1929. The Oban-Melfort-Ford and return service made up part of a circular tour to Loch Awe and back to Oban by train (which could be made in either direction), the other service being from Oban to Taynuilt via Connel. Both services were provided by the same vehicle, an Albion 'Viking Six' motor bus, registration UR 3749, which was painted in LMS livery with LMS on its sides in shaded lettering. The service did not last long in that guise, being withdrawn at the end of the 1931 summer season, but it reappeared in 1932, operated by W. Alexander & Sons (which was by then a subsidiary of SMT in which the LMS had a financial stake).

Even larger than Loch Awe is, of course, Loch Lomond, the largest freshwater loch in the United Kingdom. The steamers there were jointly owned by the CR and NBR, ownership passing to a joint LMS and LNER committee in 1923, by which time there were six railway-owned steamers operating on the loch: *Empress*, which dated from 1888, *Prince George* and *Princess May*, which had been added to the fleet in 1899, *Prince Edward of* 1911, the largest of the fleet, and *Queen Mary* and *Princess Patricia*, which were acquired in 1914, and which had previously sailed on the River Thames as *Earl Godwin* and *Shakespeare*. *Queen Mary* was sold about 1932, leaving five steamers operating. However, motor bus competition took its toll on the viability of a steamer service and the winter service was discontinued altogether from 1933, although, conversely, tram (until 1928) and bus competition seems to have considerably boosted the summer traffic on the loch. By 1939 only two steamers, *Prince Edward* and *Princess May*, were still in service and it seemed that they could not long survive. However, the major reduction in Clyde Coast services resulting from the war, and the associated public anxieties about safety on the Clyde in wartime, resulted in a major boost for excursions on safe inland waterways. The two ageing steamers unexpectedly found themselves carrying up to half a million passengers each year! Such golden days could not last, of course, and the post-war years saw a significant drop in passengers, by nearly 50% in 1946. *Prince Edward* and *Princess May* lasted until in 1953 the considerably larger *Maid of the Loch* entered service, *Princess May* being withdrawn immediately, with *Prince Edward* following two years later.

The interior of the camping coach at Biggar in the 1930s, showing the basic facilities – they were seen as substitutes for camping, not hotels. The corridor is visible, one of the LMS's marketing claims being that for its camping coaches clients could move from the communal areas to their sleeping quarters without going outside. The oil lamp reminds us that this was an era long before the universal availability of mains electricity.
(Niall Ferguson's Collection)

Life under the LMS

The LMS had many associated staff organisations, some of them sponsored or supported by the company, others of less direct interest to it. The ambulance groups had been around for many years, as had the Mutual Improvement Classes for engineers, and some of the associations, such as those related to horticulture, were indirectly supported by the railway through the station garden competitions and the like.

The Northern Division had its own football league, rather more widespread than the Caledonian Railway could have mustered. The results of the 1930-31 league are in the table; the teams and their names are the most interesting feature, although by this time teams such as Wordies' Athletic and St. Rollox Thistle had disappeared.

The LMS Temperance Union was a fairly obvious society for the time, less so the LMS Fur and Feather Club, but the sporting groups were understandably widespread. Others included the LMS (Glasgow) Choir, LMS Rovers and Scouts, LMS (Glasgow) Ladies Swimming Club and the St. Rollox Works Male Voice Choir but the Midland Dining Car Sick Club sounded less appealing.

In 1930 the erstwhile Caledonian 4-2-2 No.123, now renumbered LMS No.14010 and repainted in red livery, was returned to revenue-earning service from its recent use on officers' specials, and was regularly used on passenger working between Perth and Dundee. This was usually on quite

	Played	Won	Lost	Drawn	For	Goals Against	Points
Signal &Telegraph	16	15	1	0	60	17	30
Stirling Loco	16	13	2	1	58	14	27
Greenhill	20	12	5	3	55	21	27
Strathaven Strollers	17	10	3	4	47	22	24
Circle Amateurs	17	11	4	2	49	30	24
L M S Electrical	19	10	5	4	47	37	24
Smithy Lye	17	9	4	4	38	24	22
Kilmarnock C&W	18	8	9	1	44	49	17
Carstairs LMS	9	7	1	1	36	4	15
St. Rollox	13	6	5	2	30	16	14
*Motherwell LMS	13	7	4	2	35	26	14
Balloch	18	5	10	3	25	38	13
Beattock	9	5	2	2	33	16	12
Robroyston Rovers	19	5	13	1	31	61	11
Dumbreck LMS	15	5	8	3	22	59	11
Ballochmyle LMS	15	4	10	1	22	36	9
Buchanan St. Goods	15	3	9	3	26	50	9
Pullman Car	17	1	14	2	22	51	4
Maryhill LMS	15	1	12	2	14	54	4
Central Parcels	18	1	16	1	19	88	3

* Two points deducted for playing ineligible players.

Meikle Earnock station on the Hamilton–Strathaven line. This was a mineral area and the station supervised various industrial sidings and some collieries, although some of those between here and Quarter were supervised by the latter. The station closed to passengers in 1943, a little under two years before the line lost its passenger service. The lone private-owner mineral wagon in the siding, with 'cupboard doors' once common for this type, testifies to the diminishing traffic, while the use of an old van body as a small goods store shows that this traffic never amounted to much. Note the signalman on the balcony cleaning the box windows. (David Stirling's Collection)

smartly timed trains between the two cities, rather than the stopping services, causing considerable interest from the railway enthusiast population – and others, for the general public was more aware of railways then than it is now. This occasioned some correspondence in the enthusiast press and in more august organs, and there were calls for the engine to be retained rather than broken up. The suggestions that this locomotive be retained were extended to other notable survivors from the past. In a letter to *The Times* published on 2nd April 1932 Harold Hartley stated that Sir Josiah Stamp had given instructions that No.14010 and the ex-LNWR 2-4-0 *Hardwicke* were not to be broken up. It was noted that No.14010 had run over 40,000 miles in the previous two years.

By late 1934 No.14010 had stopped hauling the fast trains between Perth and Dundee, it was reported, but was noted as being relegated to working as station pilot at Perth, on which its struggled because of its limited adhesion, and on piloting duties from Perth shed. No.14010 was withdrawn for preservation in 1935, by then being the last active single driving axle locomotive in the country. Happily it is still with us in the Glasgow Transport Museum.

In January 1931 'arrangements', a euphemism for charges, were made for the parking of cars, three-wheeled vehicles and motor cycles at stations. The LMS was certainly modern with its use of publicity 'spin'.

Football was a source of revenue in the LMS period in a way that has changed beyond all recognition. Before the days of television those interested had to go to the matches, and until private motor cars were common that meant going by public transport. For short journeys that might be by tram or bus, but for longer distances the train remained dominant. More local matches might involve thousands of spectators, but the internationals were on a grand scale: the Scotland v England International at Hampden Park in Glasgow in March 1931 was attended by about 130,000 people, many of them travelling there by train. 218 special trains were laid on for the event, from all over the UK, sixteen of them from south of the Border. Three arrived in Buchanan Street station from Inverness and Wick early in the morning, followed by others from Blair Atholl, Aberdeen, Dundee and Oban, while St Enoch had trains from Annan, Dumfries, Kircudbright, Portpatrick and Whithorn. (The LMS did not mention any that might have come by the LNER!) Mount Florida and Kings Park stations were both close to the stadium and shared the traffic, the lion's share going to Mount Florida. Kings Park had fourteen trains on its down line, from Maryhill and places in the Clyde Valley, these being sent forward on to the Lanarkshire & Ayrshire line and stabled in the yards at stations like Whitecraigs or Patterton, while in the opposite direction six specials off the L&A called at Kings Park and were stabled at Carmyle. Mount Florida had a more intensive service, which commandeered four platforms at Glasgow Central, the East Kilbride trains being diverted to St. Enoch for the duration to make room. Forty-one specials were run round the Cathcart circle to Mount Florida, the empty stock trains having been run into Central in pairs to reduce line occupancy. For the return traffic Kings Park saw the reverse of what happened when the people arrived, but at Mount Florida twenty trains were stacked nose to tail in the section south of the station and dispatched to Central as soon as they had been loaded and the previous one had cleared the section ahead. St. Enoch and Buchanan Street then had their own services to dispatch. This was made more complicated by there still being a mix of the vacuum and Westinghouse brakes, so engines had to be matched to trains of the right brake.

The LMS, following the earlier example of the LNER and GWR, introduced camping coaches in 1934, making some play of its use of converted bogie corridor vehicles, allowing the occupants to move from the living quarters to the bedrooms without going outside, as they had to in the compartment vehicles used for the earliest examples.

Caledonian Personalities

The LMS took over more than just some physical assets – it also inherited the Caledonian Railway's staff. Many of the CR men went on to higher things under the LMS, while for those less in the limelight there were in due course opportunities for promotion to posts on the other sections of the LMS. There was mobility between the Scottish sections, but at a modest rate, many staff tending to stay in the area where they had started.

Donald Matheson became Deputy General Manager for Scotland under the LMS, but enjoyed this position for only a short time until he retired at the end of 1926. Matheson moved to the CR from the engineering contractor for the Glasgow Central Railway, becoming the CR's engineer then General Manager, before effectively continuing that role (but not the title) for the LMS Northern Division.

John Ballantyne had been the CR's Chief Goods Manager since 1918, becoming General Superintendent (Northern Division) of the LMS on 1st January 1923, but he soon moved to be Chief Goods Manager for the whole LMS at Euston. By 1942, although retired, he was the Scottish chairman of the Railway Benevolent Institution.

The Caledonian's Locomotive Superintendent, William Pickersgill, was appointed LMS Divisional Mechanical Engineer at St. Rollox. He was then 63 years of age and retired to Bournemouth in 1925, where he had a sadly short retirement, dying on 2nd May 1928. Pickersgill was succeeded in Scotland by another former Caledonian employee, John Barr, CR Assistant Superintendent (Running), who became Divisional Superintendent (Motive Power).

Robert Killin, who had been the CR's Superintendent of the Line, was promoted by the LMS first to the Midland Division, returning to Scotland in 1924 to become General Superintendent of the Northern Division, with Malcolm Speir as his assistant. By mid 1925, Killin, now CBE, became a JP for Lanarkshire, and later took on the role of chair of the Glasgow board of David MacBrayne (1928) Ltd.

Malcolm Speir, whose career started on the Midland Railway, joined the Caledonian in 1912 as Outdoor Assistant General Superintendent. On the LMS he became Assistant General Superintendent, Northern Division. In 1931 he became Secretary and General Manager of the Northern Counties Committee of the LMS in Northern Ireland, returning to be Chief Officer for Scotland in 1941.

Late in 1931 Irvine Kempt, the Carriage & Wagon Superintendent for Scotland, retired, removing a famous name from the scene. Sharing a name with his better-known father, Kempt started as an apprentice locomotive engineer at St. Rollox in 1888, and became Assistant Superintendent of Works (Locomotive and C&W) in 1914.

W. Yeaman joined the CR in 1903 and became Chief Clerk in the Goods Manager's Office in 1911, then under the LMS Chief Clerk to the Divisional Goods Manager (in the Northern Division), then Indoor Assistant in 1925 and Assistant Goods Manager in 1927 before moving to Leeds and to Euston in 1931. In the following year he became Commercial Manager for Scotland.

This understates the CR's influence, for in 1928 the LMS President, Sir Josiah Stamp, noted that between a quarter and a fifth of the chief officers at Euston were Scots, though no doubt not all had moved there in 1923.

David Gibson, the Caledonian Railway's celebrated driver of *Cardean* for many years and later of other CR locomotives and the 'Royal Scot' No.6127 *Novelty,* on which he performed various exploits, retired in November 1929 and died on 26th December 1943. Gibson was based at Polmadie for his entire driving career. He was a celebrated figure, more than his post might suggest, and when he retired at the age of 65 both Robert Killin, General Superintendent of the Northern Division, and John Barr, Superintendent of Motive Power (Northern Division), turned out to mark the occasion and wish him well.

Lambie 4-4-0T No.15024 in front of Dewar's distillery at the north end of Perth station. Each of the three pre-grouping partners in Perth joint station had maintained its own pilot engines at the station, which was the scene of massive amounts of shunting as through carriages were transferred from one train to another. The tracks in the background were the former North British Railway goods yards. (J. G. Coltas)

Road Hauliers

Instead of using its own staff to transport goods to and from the railway depots, the Caledonian Railway sub-contracted that function to the independent firm of Wordie & Company. Wordie & Co. had signed its first railway haulage contract with the Edinburgh & Glasgow Railway in 1842, and by 1923 as well as providing cartage for most of the Scottish railway companies, including the Caledonian, it also had contracts with many of the shipping fleets working on the west coast of Scotland. Therefore in 1923 Wordie & Co. became cartage agents in Scotland for not only the LMS but also the LNER. Even in the 1930s cartage was mainly horse-hauled with Wordie's stables in Dundee alone holding over 200 horses, but motor traffic increasingly took over the work, as maintaining such numbers of animals became more and more expensive. Wordie's had first used motor lorries in 1905 in Glasgow and the additional powers obtained by railway companies to operate road services in 1928 increased the rate of change. Wordies used motor vehicles from an early date in Perth, Stirling and Aberdeen, and in 1924 a 2½-ton Leyland lorry was transferred to Perth from Dundee, where there were already two other motor vehicles.

1930 sounded the warning for the horse, however, as in that year the Karrier Cob 'mechanical horse' was introduced, built specifically at the request of the LMS, to provide an economical alternative to the horse, with reduced running and maintenance costs, a higher average speed, but

An early Scammell 'mechanical horse' when they were new, being used to demonstrate what they were capable of. Clearly the driver needed to judge carefully between showing off the small turning circle of his steed and retaining its load. (David Stirling's Collection)

equal manoeuvrability. 1933 saw the introduction of the better-known Scammel Mechanical Horse and in 1937 Karrier brought out its Bantam which was available both as a tractor and as a 4-ton platform lorry. Wordie's acquired one at Aberdeen in 1937, a second following in 1939, with that depot having eighteen Bantams by 1948.

The year 1932 saw Wordie's come completely under the control of the LMS and that, together with the 1928 Act, saw an acceleration of the change to motor transport, with diesel power being increasingly used, especially after the war, when large quantities of 8-ton ex-military ERF lorries fitted with AEC 7.7 litre six-cylinder diesel engines became available. By the late 1930s the LMS was advertising not only its usual collection and delivery service in towns but also a 'country lorry service' at reduced rates from rural stations other than in the least populated areas.

The nationalisation of the railways also saw the end of Wordie's. The family had sold their last remaining shares to the LMS in 1947 and, as a wholly-owned subsidiary, Wordie & Co. became Wordie & Co. BTC until it changed its name to become part of British Road Services in 1950

Loch Awe station looking westwards. The pier was on the left, beside the station, while Loch Awe Hotel is just visible through the trees on the right. Loch Awe was served by the Glasgow–Oban trains and the Dalmally–Oban local, but in some timetables there was a Loch Awe–Oban train to satisfy the demand from passengers from the steamers returning to Oban. The signal box was a later addition, in 1902, close to the site of an earlier ground frame. Note the lift connecting the platform with the hotel, also the channel point rods in the left foreground: the LMS spent some effort renewing the round ex-CR point rods with the channel design in the 1920s and 1930s. (J. L. Smith/ The Lens of Sutton Collection, negative 51347)

Gleneagles Hotel

The Caledonian Railway, as with most railway companies, also owned a chain of hotels operated, and often constructed, in conjunction with its major stations. Probably the most famous of these was the hotel in Edinburgh, constructed above Princes Street station, which competed for grandeur and prominence with the North British Railway's hotel above Waverley station at the other end of Princes Street. There was also a large and successful hotel adjacent to Glasgow Central station, while the company jointly owned the station hotel at Perth.

In 1909 Donald Matheson, General Manager of the Caledonian Railway, conceived the idea of building a large hotel in the countryside, choosing a location near Auchterarder, close to where the Crieff branch left the main line south of Perth, the station there changing its name from Crieff Junction Station to Gleneagles, after the hotel. Matheson's idea was to have a resort hotel, where wealthy guests could relax playing golf, shooting and fishing. Construction started in 1913 but was halted by the war. The two golf courses opened in 1921 but the hotel itself did not open until June 1924, and even then only in part, as the west wing was not completed until 1925. Gleneagles Hotel was designed by James Miller, an architect whose designs were used by the Caledonian Railway for many of its stations and who had also designed the Peebles Hydro and Turnberry Hotels, with Matthew Adam deputising for him after the war.

The Caledonian Railway decided only in February 1923 (it will be remembered that it did not formally join the LMS until July of that year) that it would actually own and control the hotel, a decision made partly because the golf courses had proved to be an important source of traffic and revenue.

When completed the new hotel was certainly a most imposing building. There were 215 bedrooms sleeping 350 guests but, of course, the hotel's opulence was most obvious in its public rooms. Most striking of those was the sun lounge on the south side, which was half-moon in shape with circular windows. The ballroom had a sprung floor which could accommodate 200 couples, as well as a stage with associated equipment and dressing rooms. There was a very up-to-date French restaurant *(The Fleuri)* as well as a dining hall seating 250.

Apart from the two golf courses, there were also nine hard tennis courts, which were sunk 20ft below ground level to protect players from the wind, a swimming pool, and croquet and bowling lawns.

Completion of the internal arrangements was put in the hands of Arthur Towle (formerly the Director of Hotels of the Midland Railway) and R. W. Turier, Manager of the Adelphi Hotel in Liverpool, was appointed as Manager, administration being arranged in conjunction with the Adelphi Hotel, which Turier continued to manage. Arthur Towle became the LMS's Controller of Hotels, Refreshment Rooms, and Restaurant Cars in February 1925.

Turier and Towle's involvement with Gleneagles Hotel resulted in a coincidence which became one of the main reasons for its public fame. In the years immediately after the Great War a musical group, consisting of two violinists and a pianist, calling themselves the Variety Three was touring the North of England. The trio broke up that year and the group's pianist, earned a living playing in cinemas until, in 1922, he heard that a dance band in Manchester was looking for a relief pianist. On New Year's Eve the band was playing to an audience which included Arthur Towle, and the pianist so impressed him that he was offered permanent employment at the Midland Hotel in Manchester, a job which also involved leading a small orchestra. When Gleneagles was being fitted out, Towle asked the pianist to assist in purchasing suitable pianos for the hotel. By the time Towle became controller of the LMS hotels the pianist had become Musical Director at the Adelphi Hotel and suggested to Turier and Towle that radio broadcasts would be a good way to advertise the new hotel. They agreed and asked him to take an enlarged orchestra from the LMS hotel in Manchester to Scotland. Thus on 4th June 1924 the orchestra broadcast from Gleneagles on the hotel's opening night, conducted by the pianist, Henry Hall. On Thursday 31st July 1930 Hall made his first late night broadcast from Gleneagles and from then onwards Henry Hall and his Gleneagles Band were broadcasting practically every week. When the Gleneagles Hotel closed during the winter months, the band would transfer to either the Adelphi Hotel in Liverpool or the Midland Hotel in Manchester. Gleneagles Band broadcasts attracted a lot of comment as the band was small for a regular broadcasting unit – about six musicians – but could hold an unseen audience for 90 minutes without a vocalist. Its signature tune was *Come Ye Back to Bonnie Scotland* and the broadcasts became a regular Sunday evening event right through until 1932 when Hall became conductor of the BBC Dance Orchestra.

On Christmas Eve 1935 the Caledonian Curling Club held a Grand Match, or Bonspiel, at Carsebreck, an obscure stopping place between Greenloaning and Blackford. On that occasion there were 2,576 players at the match with about 2,000 spectators. Special trains were run from Aberdeen, Glasgow, Moffat and Stirling by the LMS and from Edinburgh and Dunfermline by the LNER, all with extra vans for the curling stones brought by the players. In addition, four ordinary trains were stopped at Carsebreck for the occasion.

Carsebreck 'station' opened in 1853, as a stopping place for those attending the occasional curling match on the nearby Carsebreck loch, but there were few visible traces of it to the passenger on the main line until 1905, when a platform was built. In that year new passenger loops, one for each direction, and an associated signal box at Carsebreck were built, and shortly afterwards the railway remodelled Carsebreck, adding long headshunt sidings on both sides and a platform on the down loop. The platform was 600ft long, without lighting or nameboards, the lack of lighting reflecting the use, with the matches over well before dusk.

So the curling platform continued its obscure existence until 1935. In that year what was to be the last Grand Match held at Carsebreck took place on Christmas Eve. In its 82-year existence Carsebreck was used on about 25 occasions, none of them advertised more than a day or two in advance.

LMS

Grangemouth station with one of the Sentinel steam rail motors. One of these was based in Grangemouth at the end of the 1920s and shuttled between there and Larbert for most of the day, filling in with some turns between Larbert and Denny in the early evening before returning to the Grangemouth run. This shows the somewhat disreputable nature of Grangemouth station, with a token overall roof incapable of holding even a Sentinel railcar. The oldest of the docks, arising from the canal, were to the left of the station, but the main part of the town lay across the road bridge on the right. The lines to the docks ran to the right of the station, behind the standing carriages. Grangemouth's passenger service consisted of the LMS local service to Larbert, LNER locals to Polmont and two or three daily through LNER trains to Glasgow. (Niall Ferguson's Collection)

7

The War and its Aftermath

The likelihood of a new European war breaking out had been apparent since the Munich crisis of 1938 and the experience of the Great War had taught both the Government and the railway companies that efficient railway communications under a central organisation would be essential for victory. Therefore in 1938 the armed services and the various government departments appointed movement officers throughout the United Kingdom who were to liaise with nominated railway officers to act as a channel of communication with the railways, to implement decisions regarding major movements, to authorise and arrange minor movements, and to facilitate the movement of essential traffic. A scheme which had initially been devised in September 1938 was, in fact, to be one of the most memorable events involving the railways in the period leading up to and immediately following the declaration of war: the evacuation of civilians (principally children) from cities. Although London is the city that most often springs to mind when evacuation is discussed, provincial cities considered to be obvious targets for enemy bombers, such as the ports of Southampton and Portsmouth on the south coast of England, were also evacuated, and in Scotland the LMS was involved in the evacuation of Edinburgh, Glasgow and Dundee, all in former Caledonian territory. It was decided that evacuation would last four days, commencing on 1st September 1939. However, far fewer people actually turned up for evacuation than was expected (approximately 50% of those anticipated). For the three Scottish cities the numbers were:

In addition 115 evacuation trains were also run from Clydebank, carrying a further 45,937 passengers. None of the above figures include empty stock working in connection with the evacuation. June 1940, of course, saw the evacuation of a large part of the British Expeditionary Force from the beaches of Dunkirk. Although the major impact of the sudden arrival of over 319,000 troops fell on the Southern Railway, those troops still had to be dispersed throughout the United Kingdom and that task was also the responsibility of the other members of the 'Big Four'. Immediately after Dunkirk troops were moved to various defence stations throughout the United Kingdom to guard against the very real threat of an invasion and, in the middle of June 1940, the garrison in Northern Ireland was strengthened when, between 16th and 19th June, 23 trainloads of troops were taken from southern England to Carlisle. From there they journeyed over the Portpatrick & Wigtownshire section to Stranraer, where they boarded ships for Larne. LMS steamers on the normal passenger sailings were commandeered for the purpose, all normal civilian sailings being cancelled. Thereafter similar transfers were made at regular intervals, the largest during the war period being in February and March 1941, when considerable numbers of personnel and mechanical transport were transferred to Northern Ireland. The number of personnel in Northern Ireland meant that from July 1940 there was a daily special train in each direction between Stranraer and Birmingham, calling at intermediate stations, supplemented from September by a second one running between Stranraer

	Number of trains			Number of passengers		
	Scheduled	Run	%	Scheduled	Carried	%
Edinburgh	61	31	51	37,068	8,601	22
Glasgow	226	207	91	160,512	77,702	44
Dundee	52	24	46	37,886	6,208	16
Total	339	262	77	235,466	92,511	39

'Coronation' Class 4-6-2 No.6224 Princess Alexandra *in plain wartime black livery at Polmadie on 27th October 1945. The generally run-down appearance and the wartime austerity are all too evident. In the background is the 1920s mechanical coaling plant.* (H. C. Casserley.)

and London. In addition two special trains ran each fortnight from Invergordon naval base on the coast north of Inverness, one to Glasgow and the other to London, the return journeys being made at the end of the fortnight.

With the English Channel and North Sea effectively closed to merchant shipping by German submarines, mines and aircraft, Bristol, and more particularly the Mersey and the Clyde, became the principal ports of the United Kingdom, a role which increased with the entry of the United States into the war in 1941, although the pressure was eased somewhat by the opening of the specially constructed Cairnryan Military Port. Construction of that port commenced in 1941 and it opened fully in 1943, being reached by a branch which left the Portpatrick Railway between Stranraer and Castle Kennedy, and which had opened in 1942.

The year 1944 saw the peak of the influx of American personnel and, with the Allied invasion of Europe imminent, April saw the heaviest traffic with the requirement, during one period of only seven days, for 75 empty carriage trains containing no fewer than 1,244 individual vehicles, to be worked from the South to Scotland, whilst during the same period a staggering 2,069 loaded coaches were despatched from Scotland.

The end of the war in Europe did not, however, see the end of the pressure on the west coast ports and the LMS in Scotland, as troops on the Continent, mainly British, but with a small number of Americans, were demobilised or returned on leave. The size of such movements can be gathered from the fact that 96 special trains were required from the Mersey and Clyde over four days in January 1945 to move troops from the ports to their destinations. Within a week of that another 87 trains were needed over a five-day period, with no fewer than 28 special trains being run on just one of those days.

The unpredictability of both shipping and the military meant that such movements often went awry at short notice. Of 87 trains scheduled to operate from the Clyde and Mersey over four days at the end of March 1945, the schedules for the Clyde services which had been previously agreed with the War Office were altered so that on 30th March four trains were delayed for two hours and five were postponed until the following day because of the late arrival of inbound ships, and on the 31st no fewer than seven trains were postponed for 24 hours because of a suspected case of smallpox on one of the ships.

Personnel, not always British, also moved in the opposite direction. During February and March 1945 20,000 repatriated Soviet prisoners-of-war were shipped home via the

Clyde, Belgian and Dutch troops were moved to and from training camps in Northern Ireland via Stranraer, and five trains (out of a total of 28) ran over the former Caledonian Railway to repatriate Polish troops from Central Scotland via Tilbury. The year 1945 also saw the longest run of a troop train undertaken by the LMS during the war when, on 24th March, a special train conveying four officers, 144 men and 15 tons of baggage ran from Thurso via Perth and Carlisle to Stanford-le-Hope. Although a comparatively small unit, special working was needed as accommodation could not be provided by ordinary services. The journey of 773 miles took 26½ hours, the train being worked by six different locomotives and corresponding sets of enginemen and guards.

All these movements put considerable strain on the infrastructure of the former Caledonian lines. The key point in LMS communication between England and Scotland was

obviously Carlisle and during peacetime the flow of traffic had been managed by running regular fully and partly fitted freights, however, with the outbreak of war, and particularly after the fall of France, the increased requirements of military rail movements put severe strains on the traffic, a strain which increased considerably with the partial opening of the deep-water military port at Cairnryan in 1941. Although the situation was eased by the construction of additional siding accommodation at Kingmoor Yard, the German air raids of 1940-41 brought into focus the importance of the bridge carrying the main lines over the River Eden north of the city. Should that bridge have been rendered unusable by enemy action, the only cross-border rail connections between England and Scotland would have been over the LNER's Waverley route, or by the East Coast Main Line, with a catastrophic effect on the war effort. Because of that, the Ministry of Munitions authorised the construction of a second bridge over the Eden close to the existing one, and the opportunity was also taken at the same time to relieve a pre-existing bottleneck by providing two additional lines between Carlisle No.3 and Etterby Junction signal boxes. It was also realised that, whilst damage to the West Coast line at Carlisle would leave the LNER routes as the only ones across the border, the converse was also true, and possibly more likely, the east coast being more accessible to German air raids. It

A pair of Fowler 2-6-4Ts, Nos.2418 and 2420, on a train of non-corridor compartment stock arriving in Platform 11 at Glasgow Central on 8th May 1946. No.11 was one of the long platforms at Central, indeed lengthened by the LMS for sleeper services, although placed at the western side of the station away from other the main long-distance platforms. (J. L. Stevenson)

A reasonably typical late LMS freight train, with a higher proportion of vans than at the start of the company's life, along with some containers, heading northwards near Symington behind '60' Class 4-6-0 No.14641. 17th May 1947. (J. L. Stevenson)

was felt that in such circumstances the existing route north of Carlisle would be unable to cope with the potential increase in traffic. The chief problem was the severe gradient on either side of Beattock summit (1 in 99 in the up direction and 1 in 77 in the down) and, in order to maximise freight traffic, goods loops were provided at Ecclefechan, Dinwoodie and Abington and, so as to reduce pressure on the marshalling yards at Carlisle, increased up and down siding accommodation was provided at Law Junction, enabling unmarshalled freight trains to work between Scotland and the Western and Central Divisions of the LMS without being re-marshalled at Carlisle.

Cairnryan Military Port also put considerable increased strain on the former Glasgow & South Western Railway (G&SWR) lines and, although not strictly the remit of this volume, the knock-on effect that had on the former Caledonian lines produced changes which need mentioning. Again in order to reduce marshalling at Carlisle, carriage sidings at Woodhill (near Kilmarnock) were remodelled to form an up marshalling yard capable of dealing with 290 wagons and the capacity of the existing marshalling yard at Elderslie was also increased.

The other place on the West Coast route to Scotland where the strain of wartime traffic was felt was at Glasgow Shields Junction No.1, where the main lines to and from Glasgow Central, Glasgow St. Enoch and the Clydesdale branch lines to and from the Caledonian Section via Rutherglen converged. The use of the ports at Greenock and Gourock, together with the opening of a number of munitions factories, resulted in a 75% increase in the number of freight trains that had to be dealt with at Shields Junction, and so a scheme was devised whereby an up goods loop was provided between Shields Junction No.1 and Terminus Junction signal box by using the existing reception line for Kinning Park goods depot together with the departure line from General Terminus station, by which means a burrowing junction was provided for freight trains between Shields Junction No.1 and the up Clydesdale branch line, and conflicting movements on the main line were much reduced.

The opening of new factories in Scotland producing munitions and other war material put increased pressure on the LMS in Scotland not just in connection with moving their products and the raw materials necessary for their production, but also in providing passenger transport for the workforces employed. The first new station to open was probably Muirton Halt, between Perth and Luncarty, which came into use in 1939 to serve a neighbouring War Department factory, and Ravenscraig Halt opened on 6th October 1941. The Great War had seen the movement of locomotives to locations far from their normal homes, with LNWR 2-4-0 *The Auditor* and

LSWR Adams 4-4-2 radial tanks being found on the Highland Railway and similar traffic demands during the Second World War also resulted in strange migrants being seen in Scotland. Southern Railway E4 Class 0-4-2Ts once again crossed the border, as they had in the earlier conflict, and were to be seen at various locations on former Caledonian, G&SWR and Highland Railway lines, such as at Ayr and at Cairnryan Military Port. The entry of the USA into the war produced further strange locomotives including, apart from the common 2-8-0s and 2-10-0s, a USA 0-6-0T (later famous after the war when purchased by the Southern Railway for use at Southampton Docks) which was to be found working at Lockerbie in September 1943.

As regards the actual results of enemy action, with the exception of Clydeside, the LMS lines in Scotland were fairly free of air raids. The first air raid of the war in Scotland occurred on the afternoon of 16th October 1939, when the Forth Bridge was subjected to a bomb and machine gun attack, no damage being caused. Between 1st December 1940 and 31st December 1941 there was a total of 780 air raids involving LMS property in the United Kingdom, 49 of which were in Scotland: but of those 49 no fewer than 40 were on Clydeside, accounting for 5% of the UK total, with only five raids causing significant damage elsewhere in Scotland. The three heaviest raids on Clydeside throughout the war occurred in March and May 1941. Two (on the nights of 13th/14th March and 5th/6th May) occurred on the south bank of the River Clyde, whilst the third (on the night of 6th/7th May) was north of the river. During the course of the first of these, bombs exploded at twelve locations and unexploded bombs were discovered at a further four; running lines were blocked in five places, the most serious being between Dumbarton and Dalmuir, where both up and down lines were blocked for over a week.

The first of the May raids damaged a bridge carrying LMS lines over the LNER between Dumbarton and Bowling, causing the up line to be unusable for nearly four weeks; running lines were blocked at three other places and damage to railway property occurred at a further five. During the following night running lines were blocked at four locations, but all were open for traffic again within three days.

'Black Five' 4-6-0 No.4997 at Glasgow Buchanan Street station on 23rd April 1948. Although not as steep as the exit from Glasgow's Queen Street station, trains leaving Buchanan Street faced a stiff climb, in tunnel, as soon as the station yards had been passed. Buchanan Street Station signal box is visible to the right of the locomotive. This engine was one of the final series, built in 1947 at Horwich. (H. C. Casserley)

Callander station's footbridge used to be enclosed and surmounted by this large ornamental clock, until 1947, when a runaway portion of a goods train which had stalled on the 1 in 61 through the Pass of Leny ran back to Callander and collided with a train in the station, demolishing the footbridge. Pickersgill 4-4-0 No.14485 stands in the down platform on a passenger train two years earlier, on 21st March 1945. (J. L. Stevenson.)

The LMS, of course, also had lines on the east coast of Scotland with major stations in Edinburgh, Perth, Dundee and Aberdeen, and it was not always damage to its own lines that gave the LMS operating problems. On the afternoon of 16th August 1941 German aircraft dropped high explosive bombs on the LNER's North Esk viaduct near Montrose, one of which exploded on the girders whilst a freight train was on the viaduct. The explosion derailed and damaged several of the vehicles of the train and caused damage to the viaduct which necessitated it being closed to traffic for a fortnight. During that period all traffic was diverted over the former Caledonian line between Guthrie Junction and Dubton

Junction, requiring reversal at Guthrie. Some must have wished for the former direct Friockheim Junction–Glasterlaw curve. Apart from that Scotland, fortunately, was too far away to be subjected to the intense bombardment by V1 and V2 rockets experienced by the London area in 1944 and after the autumn of 1943 there were no significant air raids north of the border.

Aftermath

The war left all the railways in the United Kingdom in a parlous state, the LMS in Scotland no less than those nearer to continental Europe. Despite the pressures to which they had been subjected, the staff had done their utmost to contribute to the war effort and it was, therefore, not surprising that Lord Royden, Chairman, and Sir William Wood, President of the LMS, sent the following message to all LMS staff, at home and in the services:

"The complete surrender of Germany has brought to a glorious conclusion the resistance of the Allied Nations to the attempts to bring under Nazi Fascist domination our liberty-loving country.

"To that great effort and in the preparation for it the whole LMSR organisation has played a really great part

The interior of a non-smoking third class 'vestibule stock' vehicle on the post-war 'Royal Scot', showing a posed shot. The tables were a welcome addition, as also was the panelling in attractive wood veneer. This is third class, so the meaning of the large 1 in the window is obscure. (LMS official photo)

Taking afternoon tea in the third class restaurant car of the post-war 'Royal Scot'. In those days the restaurant car facilities were segregated by class. (LMS official photo)

during the last six years. Alike in the movement of traffic on the line, at stations and offices, in the workshops ... we have every reason to be proud of the national services of the LMS staff."

Despite the parlous state reached by the LMS as a result both of minimising on maintenance, and of turning large parts of its production capacity over to work intended for the war effort such as munitions production, efforts were soon under way to restore normality.

The post-war Caledonian section was troubled by a couple of accidents. On 21st July 1945 a down express passenger train, headed by No.6231 *Duchess of Atholl* ran past the protecting signals at Ecclefechan and collided with a freight being shunted into the refuge siding to make way for the express. The locomotive was turned on its side and the train derailed injuring 31 passengers, but the only deaths were the driver and fireman of No.6231. Less seriously, on 8th August 1947 the 6.05am from Oban to Glasgow ran into a boulder on the track in the Pass of Brander and the locomotive and at least one carriage were derailed, fortunately without any deaths. This stretch of track was well known for the signals connected to a protecting wire fence, designed to be placed to danger by boulders coming down the mountain side, but on this occasion, in a manner unexplained, this boulder managed to evade the protection.

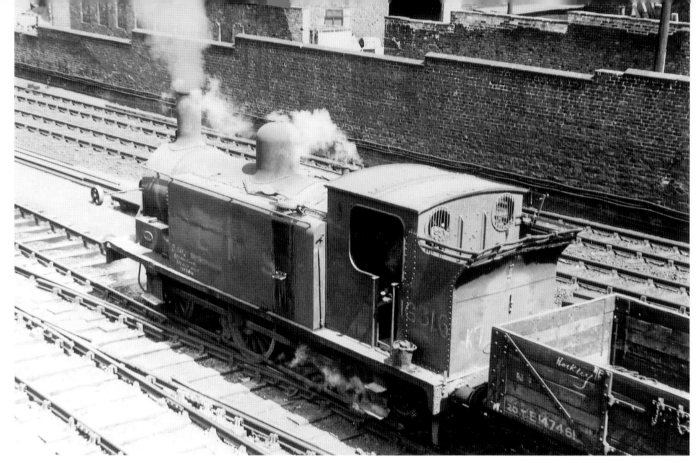

Ex-CR McIntosh 0-6-0T No.16316 on a transfer freight at Carlisle Viaduct yard in 1949, sporting graffiti and bucket, but apparently little coal. The LMS arranged some through freights between Scotland and its southern divisions, but there was still a need to exchange goods between the divisions at Carlisle, and of course to and from the LNER, although transfer freight was not what it had been in pre-grouping days. (J. L. Stevenson)

Gagie Halt on the Dundee to Forfar direct line seen in March 1961. Opened by the LMS on 2nd September 1935, the request made by Colonel Mount when he made his inspection the following year, that the planked platform was replaced with tarmac, never happened. Even at the best of times only just over twenty passengers a day used the station and boarding or alighting from a train after dark, with only oil lamps for illumination, must have been a risky business. (The late Norris Forrest)

Developments

The programme of carriage building was resumed smartly in 1945, not least because of the need to make up for war damage, but nevertheless the LMS got the process in motion faster than its peers. Between then and the end of the company's existence 2,437 carriages were built, mostly corridor compartment types, 60ft long.

In 1947 a new connection was installed at Stevenston between the former G&SWR and CR lines. The CR Ardrossan line had fallen out of use during the war, as war traffic did not use it, and rather than refurbish the entire stretch from Lugton for the somewhat sparse boat train service to Montgomerie Pier, this short spur, under half a mile long, was opened on 16th June 1947, allowing the abandonment of the CR line eastward to Kilwinning, although it still remained in use for goods traffic from Kilwinning to Lugton. Montgomerie Pier was thereafter served from the G&SWR route and the new spur. The remarkable thing about this spur is that it was the first occasion on which the LMS had needed to obtain Parliamentary authorisation for a new line in Scotland, there having been no other spurs connecting the CR and G&SWR or indeed any others.

Fairburn 2-6-4T No.2693 leaving Paisley Gilmour Street for Glasgow on Friday 26th October 1945, with clear signals ahead at Wallneuk Junction.
(H. C. Casserley)

Post-war services

The LMS had a great deal to cope with in the immediate post-war period: the railways were run down through the effects of the war, from air raids as well as intensive use, and the country was in a similar position, with rationing remaining in force for some years. Services did not bounce back to what they had been. This was not helped at all by a fuel shortage in the winter of 1946–7, which not only disrupted the services but caused severe difficulty with the coal supply. Some locomotives were converted to oil burning at the Government's behest (and with its financial support). These were hastily converted back to coal when it became available again, as oil was significantly more expensive than coal. There were service cancellations as a result. The gloomy tone of the time can be gleaned from the questions in the 1946 pamphlet *The LMS Answers Your Questions* about the lack of cleanliness, restaurant cars, seat reservations and slower journeys than before. Nevertheless, the company announced a £140million investment plan to improve train control, build new locomotives, carriages and wagons, and renew track and stations.

In October 1947 the LMS's last timetable showed the traditional two daytime trains, no longer named, between London and Glasgow, one taking 8 hours 50 minutes and the other 9 hours 5 minutes. There was one Birmingham–Scotland and two daytime Lancashire–Glasgow/Edinburgh services. Overnight provision was more as it had been, with three sleepers from Euston to Glasgow, one via Kilmarnock, and others to Inverness, Oban and Perth, but Euston no longer had through services, day or night, to Edinburgh, Aberdeen or Dundee. Within Scotland there were similar decelerations to those on the Anglo-Scottish services, the fastest Glasgow–Aberdeen run taking 3 hours 53 minutes. The days of the streamliners seemed a long time ago.

The passenger services on the secondary and branch lines remaining after the war reflected what had been offered in 1938, but only in a pale image. Services were generally slower and slightly fewer. The Dumfries–Lockerbie line had four trains daily, with no through carriages to or from Edinburgh. The Peebles service had shrunk less, with four trains to Peebles and five return, one working through to Glasgow in the morning, and some others to Carstairs. Muirkirk, on the other hand, had a fourth daily train where there had previously been three, though the through Lanark–Coalburn trains had gone, while services on the original Lesmahagow Railway line to Brocketsbrae were barely hanging on. Gourock still had a good service of 25 trains, about the same as 1925 but nothing like the service immediately before the war. Oban retained much the same basic service as before, while the lines around Crieff and in Angus had thinned their offerings, although Crieff retained a through carriage from Edinburgh in the afternoon and to both Edinburgh and Glasgow in the morning. Alyth had had its service thinned to the point of uselessness and Blairgowrie sported only two trains a day plus two Saturday extras to Dundee, a far cry from the smart service it had once enjoyed.

Although some of the branch lines were clearly on their last legs or simply hopeless commercially, the LMS did not start a programme of passenger closures after the war, but the raft of closures instituted in 1951-2 by British Railways, once it had established itself, shows that some culling of branch lines was probably overdue.

LMS

8

The Legacy

The 1946 Transport Bill, which received its Royal Assent on 6th August 1947, nationalised the four main British railway companies and 54 of the remaining smaller railway companies, as well as most canals, docks and road transport undertakings, into one national network – or at least that was the theory. As Michael Bonavia has related, things were not as integrated as that might suggest. For a start there were the two bodies, the British Transport Commission and the Railway Executive, with what turned out to be less than desirable clarity as to which was in charge of what. The railways were divided into Regions and, in an echo of 1923, there was much discussion at a late stage about what these should be. In England there were five Regions, corresponding roughly to the previous 'Big Four' companies, but with the LNER divided into two Regions, Eastern and North Eastern.

It was decided in addition that Scotland should become an autonomous Region of British Railways, the LMS and LNER in Scotland merging as part of that process. The most noticeable immediate effect of this was that the locomotives and rolling stock of the two companies were pooled, so that LNER locomotives and carriages were seen on former LMS lines and *vice versa*. Before a final decision was reached on the manner in which locomotives were to be renumbered another scheme reminiscent of the first days of the 1923

A pair of Fairburn 2-6-4Ts (Nos.2270 and 2271) at Dalry Road mpd shortly after the demise of the LMS, on Saturday 24th April 1948. The route indicator shows No.2270 to be due to take out a Carstairs train. (H. C. Casserley)

Kirriemuir was one branch terminus whose layout was somewhat awkward in not having a rounding loop in the platform. Here 0-4-4T No.15198 is drawing the branch train off classmate No.55161 after arrival, all amid much escaping steam. (J. L. Stevenson)

Grouping appeared, with St. Rollox in particular applying a letter 'M' prefix to all existing numbers, rather than adding 40000 to the existing number, as was done on the Highland section. Thus the former Caledonian and North British lines, along with the smaller Scottish companies, came at last under common management.

So what did the LMS leave behind, and was the erstwhile Caledonian section better or worse off as a result of its late owner? The immediate impression is the general one of a railway that had just suffered a war and was in many parts suffering from the effects of road competition, but those conditions were well beyond the LMS's control and affected the rest of the railway network too. What had the LMS achieved?

From the passenger's viewpoint, the main line services had been greatly improved before the war, both in speed and quality, while the secondary lines had shared in that improvement to a lesser extent. Services close to cities on the whole improved in frequency, but not those in rural areas. The overall quality of the rolling stock in which passengers were carried also improved: by 1948 there were no six-wheeled carriages in use, and almost no four-wheelers, the exception being the Balerno stock of later Caledonian days which still lingered on some Leith services. The bogie stock still included some once fine, but now dated, pre-grouping specimens and much LMS-built stock. Some services, mostly rural or short branches within urban areas, had closed and their clientele clearly did not enjoy those benefits, but the remaining services, and most *did* remain, had advanced since 1923. The post-war passenger speeds did not get close to the best of the late 1930s, but they were at least up to the speeds of the mid-1920s (after the slowing of the previous war had been eliminated) and the frequency of services, at least on the more successful lines, was better. The post-war recovery was not immediate: for example 'The Royal Scot', which had lost its title during the war, did not regain it until February 1948 – an easy and inexpensive point for British Railways to score. In some cases it was left to British Railways to restore facilities as the economic situation improved.

Longer-distance freight services had been much improved by the LMS, with the introduction of fast freight, fully or partially fitted with automatic brakes. On the main lines there were improvements in certain types of wagon to permit faster running. The local trip working, however, which in the case of mineral working had been a great, if primitive, revenue earner, had not changed much in nature but had shrunk a great deal in extent. Although the main freight handling had seen some, albeit rather limited, improvement, the LMS was quite innovative in some aspects, for example, it

had developed containers, including containers for furniture removals, as a means of reducing the amount of handling of the load. Some of this had reflected the growing strength of road competition, particularly for small consignments. All the railways, not just the LMS, had been steadily losing ground to road haulage throughout the period.

The LMS as a business had not been healthy either; figures for traffic showed a steady decline. That was in the face of strict economy, some wage reductions, and some investment by the LMS. Despite that, traffic declined over the period by about 15%, while the operating ratio was much the same: in fact by 1937 it had recovered some of the ground lost up to 1929, despite the effects of the intervening Depression. The war, of course, did not help, the Government paying the railways significantly less than most observers would agree was a fair price for what they carried. Nationalisation simply allowed the Government of the day to avoid paying proper compensation, and the price paid to the shareholders reflected the stock exchange valuation in 1945–6, terms which, according to Michael Bonavia, Sir Ronald Matthews of the LNER claimed "would bring a blush of shame to the leathery cheek of a Barbary pirate". LMS ordinary shareholders received £29.50 of British Transport 3% stock for each £100 of LMS stock, better than the £7.31 for LNER preferred ordinary, but nothing like the GWR's £59.06 or the Southern's £77.62. In business terms the legacy of the LMS to its shareholders was not good.

Drummond 'Jumbo' 0-6-0 No.17269 at Balornock shed on 19th February 1950. Still in LMS livery two years into the British Railways era, the number has a small letter 'M' above, an experimental method of numbering locomotives in the various regions which was later abandoned. The engine is showing its age, with extensive patching on the tender, which is vacuum piped, presumably swapped with another locomotive's. (H. C. Casserley)

The revenue was the main determinant of the dividend and, in turn, the stock valuation, but how had the equipment of the railway fared? The company had inherited a diverse collection of locomotives and rolling stock, as well as property, from a variety of companies, the Caledonian amongst them. By the end of its existence the LMS had introduced some modern locomotives, produced early in its life and based on pre-existing designs, followed by a fleet of modern, standard locomotives. Small classes of locomotives, or those judged expensive to maintain, were eliminated. Although the Caledonian locomotives were far from exempt from this purge, the 4-6-0 classes suffering badly from it, there were 736 ex-CR locomotives still in the fleet in 1947, plus a small number built by the LMS to Caledonian designs. The main services were, however, dominated by the more modern and efficient LMS types. There were also diesel shunters in some numbers, and two main line diesel locomotives were completed as the company expired. Therefore locomotive stock had been considerably improved, and the LMS bequeathed to its successors a fleet of standard locomotives on which British Railways, ignoring the benefits of more modern traction, would base its own standard types.

The carriage fleet, too, was greatly improved with much standard stock, built during the course of three design phases, and including a very prompt restart to re-equipping after the war. In this case there was a partial change in style, with the introduction of some stock with an open layout rather than with discrete compartments. It was in the ancillary stock, however, that the biggest change was evident. There had been dining cars in service before the LMS, particularly on the

Midland and LNWR, but the LMS built more than 330 catering vehicles, greatly extending their availability and redeploying the best of the older catering vehicles on secondary services. For the most part the ex-CR catering vehicles were used off the CR lines. Sadly, the most attractive ex-CR Pullman vehicle, the observation car *Maid of Morven*, neither survived nor was replaced, although BR reintroduced observation cars to the Oban line for a while. Sleeping car services, too, were increased by the LMS, which built over 250 such vehicles. In that the LMS did rather better than its peers, for its provision was noticeably greater than the others, particularly the LNER: in 1947 the LMS had 61% of the nation's sleeping cars whereas it had only 41% of the total carriage stock. It is perhaps appropriate that, as we write, all the surviving Anglo-Scottish sleeper services run to and from Euston. Again there was a resemblance between the LMS products and what BR produced with its Mark I coaches, although the Mark I vehicles were a few feet longer and fully steel framed. As with the locomotives this continuation was not just a result of LMS influence – the other main companies, with the partial exception of the Southern, whose emphasis was on electrification, had been producing similar products.

Fairburn 2-6-4T No.2242 of 1946 leaving the middle part of Glasgow Central on 29th April 1948. The arrangement of Central station was ingenious in matching long main line platforms at either side of the station with much shorter ones in the centre for local services, allowing room for the necessary pointwork before the Clyde bridges.
(H. C. Casserley)

Auchterarder station, a fairly typical wayside Caledonian station, shown here in the 1930s, looking towards Perth. The station was not close to the town it served and the railway advertised that Gleneagles also served Auchterarder, essentially showing that the passenger traffic would be vulnerable to road competition, which it duly was. The neat and tidy appearance of the station and the topiary are notable and not unusual for the time, while the wooden footbridge and the oil lighting on the platforms were common over much of the system. The substantial stone building at such a small station marks out the early opening date, as wayside stations opened later received much less elaborate structures. (J. L. Smith/The Lens of Sutton Collection, negative 51017)

We have seen that the LMS did very little in the way of station improvements on the former Caledonian Railway. It provided some good contemporary station buildings further south, but the Caledonian had already left many excellent stations and, apart from a reasonable but uninspired improvement at Buchanan Street station, there is little to say about stations. Equally the civil engineering moved generally forwards, without being particularly inspiring. The LMS did, however, seem to have a penchant for changing the signage of its predecessors, even to the extent of changing many of the signs warning people against trespass. Some of this made business sense, but to do the same for such notices, and even to appear to be trying to change history, by producing replacement plates for some locomotives which claimed that they had been built by the LMS in the nineteenth century, seems more obsessive. On the signalling and safety front the LMS again did not claim the limelight but, while it did not make spectacular progress, unlike the LNER with its introduction of relay interlocking as a means of controlling signalling, it did make progress. On the Caledonian there was

little pressing need for improvement, as CR signalling in 1923 had been perfectly satisfactory, but at a time when other companies were demonstrating pilot installations and making more sound than action, the LMS did move forward in the late 1930s with a programme of installing block controls on its main lines, including the former CR. That involved fitting track circuits in the rear of the home signal at most locations between Glasgow and Carlisle, with more complete protection against signalmen's oversights at selected places. The programme was not universal, but it went much farther than the other companies. This is perhaps symptomatic of the LMS: it got on with the job without too much fuss or publicity.

The LMS in Scotland took over three railway companies and was under severe economic pressure. How did it fare in rationalising its inheritance? There was little scope for rationalising with the Highland, and not much more with the Glasgow & South Western. Something was achieved with the latter, particularly in Galloway where more sensible working was obvious and easy. Removing the duplication of CR lines to Ayrshire was partially successful, although the CR line to Kilwinning lingered until 1947, and something might have been done in Glasgow to allow St. Enoch's traffic to use Central on Sundays. Curiously the company was more successful in rationalising arrangements with the old North British, through various closer working arrangements. This was productive, though it is easy to see things that might have been done better under unified management – running between Oban and Glasgow via Ardlui, for example – but it is notable how long these things took to establish even when the railways did come under one management. Some of the lines that were still open at the end of the LMS period were on their last legs and others, such as the main line between Perth and Aberdeen, involved costs that would prove a problem even for British Railways. More might have been done to modernise and to use the best of competing provision, but that is easy to say with hindsight, less easy to do in the real world. One cannot help agreeing with Bonavia's comment in *The Four Great Railways* that more would probably have been achieved earlier had the NB and CR come under unified management sooner.

On the waters of the River Clyde, however, there was rationalisation. This was easy for the ex-CR and ex-G&SWR fleets, where there had been a pooling and rationalisation arrangement since 1909, and unified ownership could only make things simpler. The partial takeover of MacBrayne's in 1928 and of Williamson's in 1935, allowed further progress, while there was an understanding, if not integration, with the LNER. When British Railways took over, the LMS had already done most of the rationalisation, and had modernised its fleet, consisting of nine ships and some ferries, so it was natural that the Caledonian Steam Packet Company was the body to continue running the Clyde services other than those operated by MacBrayne's. So the Caledonian name lived on into the era of the nationalised railway and indeed beyond, for when the shipping services were removed from railway control and combined with those of MacBrayne in 1973 the name adopted, Caledonian MacBrayne, continued the railway company's name to the present day.

There were other forms of rationalisation that, although not fashionable in Britain, the LMS might have achieved. In 1927 the LMS and LNER took a 50% share in the dominant Scottish motor transport company, SMT. That should have given the potential for good road-rail integration, the elimination of waste and possibly proper connections with buses in places where branch lines had been closed. None of that happened and, while the investment brought the railways a good return on their money, it did nothing for the railway business. That was a lost opportunity or perhaps, as A. J. Mullay proposes, simply one where the bus operators out-manoeuvred the railways.

As it was wont to point out, the LMS was the largest joint stock corporation in the world. It was appropriate, then, that it made some progress in modernising management methods, though there might be some lack of unanimity about how successful that was. The Executive Research Office did much work on economies in office working, and the LMS started work on improving working methods – what were later to be called 'time and motion' studies. It began a School of Transport at Derby and most significantly, in 1937, instigated the Railway Research Department there, which left its own successful legacy. Those were not developments of the CR system itself, but they left their mark on it.

On balance, then, the LMS handed over a better railway and one fitter for purpose, barring recovery from the war, than it had started with. The changes, however, were only partly visible, mainly in the area of locomotives and rolling stock, and some long-established traditions and practices were little altered. Some of the difficulties of the need for a large labour force, of slow and expensive handling of some freight, especially small loads, and of high fixed costs were left to British Railways to tackle, although the LMS had made a good start with its promotion of containers.

LMS

A group of enthusiasts on a visit to a former Caledonian steam shed in the late 1950s were watching locomotives being coaled at a three-road automated coaling plant. It will be remembered that the pre-Grouping railways had undergone two major reorganisations, the most recent of which had produced a single Region in Scotland, and nearly 35 years had passed since the first such reorganisation.

The coal available in each road corresponded to the class of locomotive to be coaled, thus the first lane had top quality steam coal for premier express locomotives, the third road had very poor quality dross, suitable only for shunting engines and such-like, whilst the middle road dispensed medium quality coal suitable for mixed traffic locomotives and the like.

The first locomotive appeared, a top link 4-6-0, and was appropriately directed to the road supplying the best coal; next came a 0-4-0ST 'Wee Pug' which received a load of poor quality coal from the third road. Then along came a former LNER V2 Class 2-6-2, most definitely a top grade of mixed traffic locomotive. Not surprisingly it started to move up the middle road when, suddenly, the coaling plant foreman appeared, made the driver reverse back and directed him into the third road, where his tender was filled with the worst quality fuel. The enthusiasts were nonplussed by this and one of them found enough nerve to ask the foreman why he had done this: "Och!", was the reply, "He's nothing but an old North British man!" Old habits die hard.

Appendices:
Opening and Closure of Lines and Stations

Lines Opened

East Kilbride–Hunthill Junction reopened 1st October 1923, closed 14th July 1924 (Greville & Spence)

Maryhill–Possil 8th January 1934, (reopened to passengers).

Connecting spur between CR and G&SWR at Stevenston 16th June 1947

Stations Opened to Passengers

Carfin Halt	1st October 1927
Croftfoot	April 1931
Drumpark	1st May 1934
East Pilton	1st December 1934
Gagie	2nd September 1935
Heath Hall Halt	1926
Hillington East	19th March 1934
Hillington West	1st April 1940
House O'Hill	1st February 1937
Kings Park	October 1928
Methven Junction	26th September 1937 (previously exchange platform)
Muirton Halt	31st October 1936
Ravelrig Halt (New Site)	1927 (For Dalmahoy Golf Course)
Ravenscraig Halt	6th October 1941
Woodhall	1938? (Dunsyre–Newbiggin)
Williamwood	8th July 1929?
Woodhall Halt	1st October 1945

Appendix 2: Lines and Stations closed by the LMS

Stations closed to passengers

		source
Botanic Gardens	6th February 1939	4
Gartsherrie	28th October 1940	4
Kelvinside	1st July 1942	4
Kirklee	1st May 1939	4
Meikle Earnock	12th December 1943	4
Mount Vernon	16th August 1943	4
Overtown	5th October 1942	4
Ravenscraig	1st February 1944	4
Strathord	13th April 1941	4

	Closed to passengers	Closed to freight	Notes	
East Kilbride–Hunthill Junction	14 July 1924	1937	One train each way Fridays only	2, 5
Cardonald–Renfrew (Porterfield)	Jun 1926	–		2
Elliot Junction–Carmyllie	2 Dec 1929	–		2
Blackwood Jct–Dunduff Quarry	–	1920s?		5
Larbert/Greenhill–Denny	28 Jul 1930	–		1, 2
Greenhill–Bonnybridge Canal	28 Jul 1930	–		1, 2
Kilwinning–Irvine (Bank Street)	28 Jul 1930	1939?		2, 5
Giffen–Kilbirnie	1 Dec 1930	1 Dec 1930		1, 2
Holytown–Morningside	1 Dec 1930	1930/47	Cleland Jct–Omoa Jct closed to all traffic, 1930	1, 2
Airdrie–Newhouse	1 Dec 1930	1 Dec 1930*	*Calderbank–Chapelhall	2
Strathord–Bankfoot	13 Apr 1931	–		1, 2
Kirtlebridge–Annan (Shawhill)	27 Apr 1931	27 Apr 1931		1, 2
Brechin–Edzell	27 Apr 1931	–	Reopened 4 Jul 1938	1, 2
Lugton–Ardrossan (local traffic)	4 July 1932	–		1
Carstairs–Dolphinton	12 Sep 1932	–	Reopened 17 July 1933	2
Tannochside–Cuilhill	–	1932?		5
Abbey Junction–Brayton	by CR	13 Feb 1933		4
Broomfield Junction–Montrose	30 Apr 1934	–	Trains diverted to LNER station	2
Dalserf–Stonehouse	7 Jan 1935	7 Jan 1935*	*Swinehill–Stonehouse	2
Larbert–Kilsyth	1 Feb 1935	1 Feb 1935	LNER continued to work Kilsyth–Banknock	2
Methven Junction–Methven	26 Sep 1937	–		1, 2
Brechin–Edzell	29 Sep 1938	–		2, 4
Elvanfoot–Wanlockhead	2 Jan 1939	2 Jan 1939		2, 4
Alton Heights Jct–Poniel Jct	11 Sep 1939	–		2
Killin–Loch Tay	11 Sep 1939	11 Sep 1939	Used for locomotives till 1965	2
Strathaven–Darvel	11 Sep 1939	11 Sep 1939	Planned closure was 25th	2
Newton–Loanend colliery	–	c1939?		5
Jerviston line (Motherwell)	–	1914/1930s		5
Law Jct–Law colliery	–	1930 part		5
Lugton–Ardrossan (through traffic)	1940?		Stevenston–Ardrossan reopened 1947.	1
Airdrie–Calderbank - works	1 Dec 1930	1941		5
Brocketsbrae–Alton Heights Jct	4 May 1942	–		2
Whifflet–Airdrie	3 May 1943	–		2
Balerno Junction–Ravelrig Junction	1 Nov 1943	–		2, 4
Carstairs–Dolphinton	4 Jun 1945	–		2, 4
Hamilton–Strathaven (via Quarter)	1 Oct 1945	–		2, 4
Stevenston–Kilwinning	–	16 Jun 1947		4
Omoa Jct–Drumbowie Jct	–	1947		5
Newmains–Langbyres Junction	–	1947		5
Mossend–Woodhall colliery	–	1940s		5
Salsburgh - east end of line	–	1940s		5
Dunsiston branch	–	1940s		5
Turdees Jct–Duntillan	–	1940s		5

Sources
1. RM April 1938, 2. contemporary *Railway Magazine*, 3. Greville & Spence, 4. Daniels & Dench, 5. Cobb

Bibliography and Sources

Sources

V. R. Anderson and G. K. Fox, *A Pictorial Record of LMS Architecture,* Oxford Publishing Co., 1981

H. N. Appleby, *Ports Owned and Served by the London, Midland and Scottish Railway,* LMS, 1932.

Michael R. Bonavia, *The Four Great Railways,* David & Charles, 1980.

Michael R. Bonavia. *British Rail: The First 25 Years,* David & Charles, 1981.

H. C. Casserley and Stuart W. Johnson, *Locomotives at the Grouping, London, Midland and Scottish Railway,* Ian Allan, 1966.

M. H. Cobb, *The Railways of Great Britain: A Historical Atlas,* Ian Allan, 2003.

J. R. L. Currie, T*he Northern Counties Railway, Vol. 2, 1903-1972,* David and Charles, 1974.

G. Daniels and L. A. Dench, *Passengers No More,* Ian Allan, 1963.

M. D. Greville and Jeoffry Spence, *Closed Passenger Lines of Great Britain, 1827-1947,* Railway and Canal Historical Society, 1974.

Chris Hawkins and George Reeve, *LMS Engine Sheds, Volume 5, The Caledonian Railway,* Wild Swan Publications, 1987.

Colin Johnston and John R. Hume, *Glasgow Stations,* David & Charles, 1979.

Graham E. Langmuir, 'Sails on Highland Lochs', *Railway Magazine,* 72, May 1933, 313–319.

A. J. Mullay, 'The LNER Coronation Express', *Backtrack,* Jan-Feb 1992, 33–36,

A. J. Mullay, 'Coronation v Coronation Scot', *Backtrack,* Mar-Apr 1992, 76-81

A. J. Mullay, *London's Scottish Railways,* Tempus Publishing, 2005

John Thomas, *The Callander & Oban Railway,* David & Charles, 1966 and 1990.

Donald Shaw, *The Balerno Branch and the Caley in Edinburgh,* Oakwood Press, 1989.

Ian Sixsmith, *The Book of the Coronation Pacifics,* Irwell Press, 1998.

L. R. Tomsett (ed), *Caledonian Railway Centenary, (1847-1947),* Stephenson Locomotive Society, 1947.

Jack W. Tyler, Notes on Outdoor Machinery Department, supplied by Stuart Rankin, some published in the *Sou-West Journal.*

Railway Magazine

LMS Magazine

CR, LMS and LNER public and working timetables

The True Line, journal of the Caledonian Railway Association

London Midland & Scottish Railway Company publications:

> *Country Lorry Service for Scottish Farms and Villages,* c1937.
>
> *A Record of Large-Scale Organisation and Management, 1923-1946,* 1946.
>
> *Grangemouth, the Scottish Port for Timber, Oil and Continental Traffic,* 1946.
>
> *The LMS Answers Your Questions,* April, 1946.

Railway Year Book